ATLAS of HORSES AND PONIES

*For Lady, Willow and Rusty, who I've never forgotten.
And with special thanks to John for teaching me so much about horses.
F. E.*

Author: Frances Evans
Illustrator: Adrienne Green
Publishing Director: Piers Pickard
Publisher: Rebecca Hunt
Editorial Director: Joe Fullman
Art Director: Andy Mansfield
Commissioning Editor: Kate Baker
Consultant: Camilla de la Bedoyere
Print Production: Nigel Longuet

Published in October 2025
by Lonely Planet Global Limited
CRN: 554153
ISBN: 978-1-83758-669-1
10 9 8 7 6 5 4 3 2 1

Printed in Malaysia

All rights reserved. No part of this publication may be reproduced, stored in a retrieval system or transmitted in any form by any means, electronic, mechanical, photocopying, recording or otherwise except brief extracts for the purpose of review, without the written permission of the publisher. Lonely Planet and the Lonely Planet logo are trademarks of Lonely Planet and are registered in the US Patent and Trademark Office and in other countries.

Although the author and Lonely Planet have taken all reasonable care in preparing this book, we make no warranty about the accuracy or completeness of its content and, to the maximum extent permitted, disclaim all liability from its use.

Stay in Touch
Lonelyplanet.com/contact

Lonely Planet Office:
IRELAND
Digital Depot, Roe Lane (off Thomas St), Digital Hub, Dublin 8, D08 TCV4, Ireland

Paper in this book is certified against the Forest Stewardship Council™ standards. FSC™ promotes environmentally responsible, socially beneficial and economically viable management of the world's forests.

Lonely planet KIDS

ATLAS of HORSES AND PONIES

illustrated by
Adrienne Green

written by
Frances Evans

CONTENTS

- 6 A World of Horses and Ponies
- 8 Atlas of a Horse
- 10 Colours and Markings
- 12 Caring for a Horse or Pony

14 North America
- 16 Canadian Horse, Morgan, American Standardbred
- 18 American Shetland, Pony of the Americas, Rocky Mountain Horse, American Saddlebred
- 20 Quarter Horse, Missouri Fox Trotter, Bashkir Curly
- 22 Cayuse Indian Pony, Appaloosa, Galiceño
- 24 *Fabulous Foals*

26 South America
- 28 Peruvian Paso, Paso Fino, Chilean Horse
- 30 Argentine Criollo, Argentine Polo Pony, Falabella
- 32 Mangalarga Machador, Campolina, Campeiro, Pampa Horse
- 34 *Donkeys, Mules and Hinnies*

36 Europe North and West
- 38 Clydesdale, Shetland Pony, Highland
- 40 Shire, Thoroughbred, Hackney
- 42 Welsh Ponies and Cobs, Irish Draught, Connemara
- 44 Icelandic, Fjord, Jutland
- 46 *Working Horses*
- 48 Swedish Warmblood, Finnish Horse, Friesian, Belgian Warmblood
- 50 Percheron, Norman Cob, Selle Francais, French Trotter
- 52 Ardennais, Breton, Boulonnais
- 54 Oldenburger, Holsteiner, Hanoverian, Haflinger
- 56 *Free-Roaming Horses*

58 Europe South and East
60 Andalusian, Lusitano, Sorraia
62 Italian Heavy Draught, Maremmano, Salerno, Murgese
64 Lipizzaner, Pindos, Skyrian
66 Shagya-Arabian, Nonius, Hucul
68 *Mythical Horses*
70 Ukrainian Saddle Horse, Trakehner, Wielkopolski, Kladruber
72 *Horse Sports*

74 Africa
76 Barb, Dongola, Bhirum
78 M'Bayar, Fleuve, Basuto, Boerperd
80 *Wild Horses*

82 Asia
84 Orlov Trotter, Don, Vladimir
86 Kabardin, Budyonny, Tersk
88 Arab, Caspian, Akhal-Teke
90 Karabakh, Karabair, Lokai, Mongolian Horse

92 *How to Talk Horse*
94 Marwari, Kathiawari, Spiti
96 Sumba, Sandalwood, Timor, Batak, Java
98 Kiso, Hokkaido, Tokara
100 *War Horses*

102 Australia and New Zealand
104 Australian Pony, Australian Stock Horse, Australian Draught
106 Brumby, Kaimanawa Horse
108 *Record-Breaking Horses*

110 Glossary
112 Index

A WORLD OF HORSES AND PONIES

Welcome to the wonderful world of horses and ponies! From the fabulous Friesian and dainty Falabella to the dashing Arab and tough Exmoor, this book will take you on an a-neigh-zing journey around the planet to meet over 100 brilliant breeds. Some are horses you might encounter at your local riding stables, while others may be less familiar.

HOW THIS BOOK WORKS

You'll find a map at the start of each chapter so you can see where the horses and ponies come from, while the profile pages give you the lowdown on each breed, their characteristics and care needs. There are also special entries that explore topics such as cute foals, horsey sports, donkeys and mules, mythical horses and much more!

It is estimated that there are around 60 million wild and domestic horses in the world today.

WHAT IS A HORSE? AND WHAT IS A PONY?

Horses are hoofed, plant-eating mammals, known for their agility, speed and strength. We're not certain exactly when horses were first tamed (or 'domesticated') by humans, but it may have been in around 4000 BCE in Central Asia. They quickly became some of our most loyal and important animal friends, helping us to farm, travel and build civilisations, carrying us into battles, and providing comfort and companionship.

Horses and ponies belong to the same species – *Equus caballus* (or the domestic horse). The main differences between horses and ponies are their shape and size. A horse has a slender build and is usually considered to be over 14.2 hands high. Ponies are smaller than this and have sturdy, stocky bodies. Some breeds, such as the Falabella and Icelandic, fall into the 'Pony' category in this book (see page 9) because they are smaller than 14.2 hands high, but they are often called small horses rather than ponies because they have the same proportions as a bigger horse, just in a little form.

WHAT IS A BREED?

A group of horses that has been deliberately bred to have the same characteristics is known as a 'breed'. Different breeds have been developed all over the world for different jobs and purposes, and they often reflect the environment that they come from.

For example, the mighty Clydesdale (1) was bred to work on Scottish farms, the dazzling Akhal-Teke (2) emerged from the deserts of Turkmenistan, and the tiny but tough Spiti (3) was developed to trek through the icy Himalayan Mountains. You can think of all the breeds you meet in this book as equine ambassadors for their home nations and cultures.

HOW CAN I MEET HORSES?

Owning a horse or pony is a dream goal for many people. But it is an enormous responsibility and a long-term commitment – a well-cared-for horse can live for 25 years or more, while many ponies live beyond 30 years. Horses and ponies need daily care, lots of space and other horsey friends to live a happy and healthy life.

There are plenty of ways to be around horses and ponies without owning one. The best place to start is your local riding centre. Here, you can learn about basic horse care and how to handle and ride a horse. You could also visit a sanctuary or rehoming centre to meet horses and ponies, and support the welfare of these beautiful animals.

ATLAS OF A HORSE

Whether they're a mighty Shire or a sturdy Shetland, all horses and ponies share the same basic features. Here's some essential horse geography.

BACK
The back is where the saddle goes when you ride a horse. It's important to know where a horse's back starts and ends so you can put your saddle in the right place – if a saddle sits too far forward (on the withers) or too far back (on the loin), this could be uncomfortable for a horse.

MANE AND FORELOCK
The long hair on the top of a horse's neck is called its mane. It protects the horse from the weather and biting insects. The piece of mane that falls between the horse's ears is called its forelock.

TAIL
A horse uses its tail for balance, to express how it's feeling and for swatting away flies.

LOIN

LEGS
A horse's front and back legs are made up of several sections:

Hock – the large joint on the back legs, located in a similar spot to the knee on the front legs

Cannon – the lower bone of a horse's leg

Fetlock – a joint that connects the cannon bone to the pastern

Pastern – the part of the leg between the fetlock and hoof, which allows the hoof to flex, and cushions the impact of each step

Elbow – the joint where the front leg meets the body

Forearm – the top bone of the front leg

Knee – the large, bending joint below the forearm

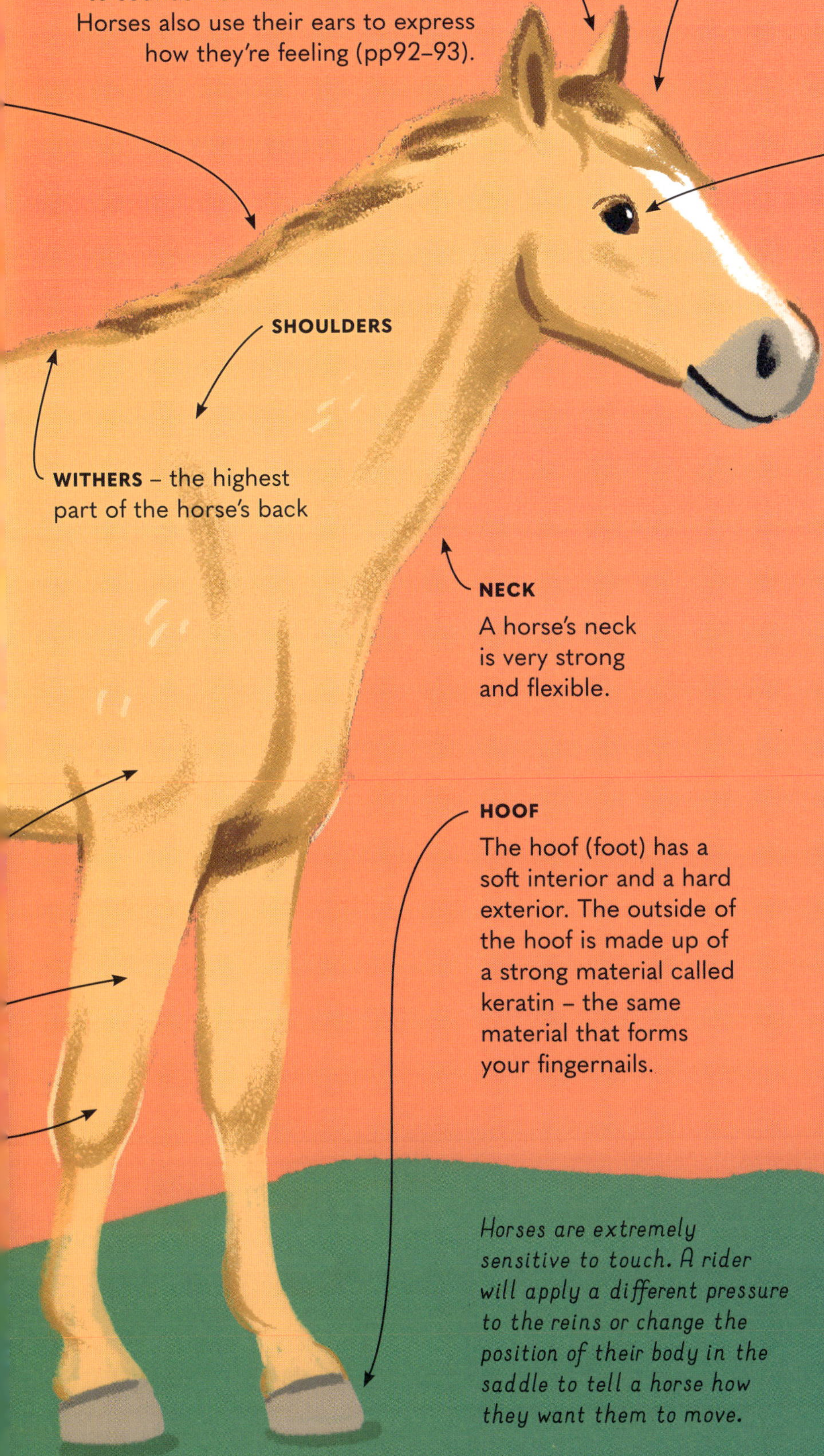

EARS

A horse has flexible, pointed ears and an incredible sense of hearing. It can swivel its ears 180 degrees to listen to sounds from different directions. Horses also use their ears to express how they're feeling (pp92–93).

HEAD

The nose, mouth and chin are called the muzzle. It is very soft and covered in whiskers that help the horse sense things close to its face. Horses use their strong sense of smell to communicate with one another and interpret their surroundings.

EYES

Horses have very big eyes that sit on each side of their head, so they can see nearly 360 degrees around. In the wild, this allows them to look out for predators without having to turn their head. They can't see immediately in front or behind them, however.

SHOULDERS

WITHERS – the highest part of the horse's back

NECK

A horse's neck is very strong and flexible.

HOOF

The hoof (foot) has a soft interior and a hard exterior. The outside of the hoof is made up of a strong material called keratin – the same material that forms your fingernails.

Horses are extremely sensitive to touch. A rider will apply a different pressure to the reins or change the position of their body in the saddle to tell a horse how they want them to move.

MEASURING HORSES

A horse's height is measured from its **withers** to the ground using a unit of measurement called a hand. One hand is equal to 10.2 cm (4 inches).

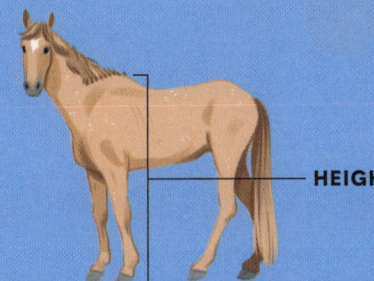

HEIGHT

HORSE TYPES

Horses can be grouped into three basic types. In this book, each breed's type is listed in its profile box:

PONY   LIGHT   HEAVY

See glossary on p110 for more information.

COLOURS AND MARKINGS

Domestic horses and ponies have an incredible range of colours and markings – from glossy chestnut and stylish black to sleek grey and even spots! Some breeds are deliberately bred to have (or not have) particular colours and markings. Here's a guide to some key colour terms.

CHESTNUT

Chestnut horses have red-brown coats, manes and tails. They may have white markings on their face and legs, but they never have any black hair.

BAY

A bay horse has a rich brown coat with a black mane, tail and legs. Bay ranges from very dark brown (almost black) to a brighter red-brown colour.

DUN

A dun horse has a tan coat with a darker mane, tail and legs. Dun horses also have a dark stripe (called a dorsal stripe) on their back and stripe markings (called zebra stripes) on their legs.

ROAN

A roan horse has a mix of white and dark hair, which gives its coat a stunning, shimmery look. For example, a black roan horse has black hair mixed with white, while a red roan has chestnut hair mixed with white.

FACE AND LEG MARKINGS

Horses and ponies have unique markings on their legs and face, which are often used as a way of telling individuals apart. Here are some common markings to look out for. These markings can appear on their own or in combinations.

FACE MARKINGS

STAR SNIP STRIP (OR STRIPE) BLAZE BALD ERMINE

SPOTTED

A spotted horse is unmistakable! This striking pattern is sometimes known as appaloosa. Appaloosa is also the name of an American breed with a spotty coat (p22).

BLACK

Black is a rare coat colour for horses as it is caused by a special gene. Some horse breeds have been deliberately bred to be all-black, such as the Friesian (p49).

GREY

Grey horses have white hair and black skin. They are born with a brown or black coat that becomes paler as they grow up until, later in adulthood, they are grey or completely white. Most horses that look 'white' are actually grey. True white horses (horses that have pink skin and are born with white hair) are very rare.

Grey horses with spots of lighter grey or white on their coats are called dappled grey.

PINTO

Pinto (also called paint or coloured) horses have coats made up of patches of white and another colour. Different colour combinations have different names. For example, a horse with black and white patches is called piebald, while a horse with patches of white and any colour other than black is skewbald.

PALOMINO AND BUCKSKIN

Palomino horses have golden coats and white manes and tails. Some palomino horses have blue eyes. Horses with golden coats and dark manes and tails are called buckskins.

LEG MARKINGS

The leg markings on a horse have different names, which reflect how much of the leg is covered.

| CORONET | HEEL | PASTERN | SOCK | HALF-STOCKING | STOCKING | HIGH-STOCKING |

CARING FOR A HORSE OR PONY

Caring for a horse or pony is lots of fun, but it is also a big responsibility. Here's a guide to the basics, so you can make sure any horse or pony you look after lives a happy and healthy life.

FOOD

Fresh grass is a horse's natural food. When that isn't available, dried grass (called hay) is the next best thing. Horses must always have access to fresh water to stay healthy. In hot weather, horses should also be given a salt block to lick, as they lose lots of salt from their bodies when they sweat.

Horses have small stomachs and need to eat little and often – in the wild, a horse will graze for about 18 hours a day. It's important to make sure your horse or pony is eating the right amount of food – too little can cause them to lose weight and too much can make them overweight and lead to health problems.

Horses can be fed small amounts of oats, barley and corn for extra nutrition in colder months, when there isn't as much fresh grass around. They can also be fed occasional vegetable and fruit treats, such as carrots.

COMPANY AND OUTSIDE SPACE

Horses are herd animals and enjoy being outside with other horses and ponies. As well as providing companionship, it's important to give your horse as much space to move around as possible. You could introduce fun activities to your horse's field, too. For example, some horses enjoy kicking a ball when they're feeling playful.

Before a horse or pony is let out into a field, the area must be checked to ensure it is free from toxic plants. A plant called ragwort is especially poisonous to horses and ponies.

SHELTER

Horses that live outdoors should always have access to a shelter, so they can escape from bad weather or flies. The shelter should be built in a dry place, away from winds, and have an entrance large enough to let all the horses in the field come and go freely.

Some horses, especially valuable sports horses, are housed in stables. This makes feeding, grooming and health checks easier. But horses are social animals and can get lonely if they are kept alone. Many pet horses are let out into a field with other horses during the day and taken into an individual stable at night, so they get the best of both worlds.

GROOMING

Most horses and ponies love being groomed (having their coats brushed). This is a brilliant way to build a bond with a horse, and it helps keep the animal's coat and skin healthy. They should be groomed each day, and before and after every riding session. As well as pampering your horsey pal, this is a good opportunity to check for injuries or signs of illness.

HOOVES AND TEETH

Like your fingernails, a horse's hooves are always growing. If you have a horse or pony, you will need to check its hooves and pick out any mud each day. Hooves must also be regularly trimmed by a farrier (someone who specialises in hoof care).

Like its hooves, a horse's teeth grow constantly. Horses and ponies should be checked by a horsey dentist every 6 months, to make sure their teeth are a healthy length.

Some horses, especially working horses or sports horses, wear metal or plastic shoes as extra protection. A farrier will check and refit a horse's shoes every 8 weeks or so to make sure the feet are in good condition and the shoes are comfortable.

NORTH AMERICA

The land of ranches, rodeos and cowboys, North America loves its horses. All modern North American breeds are descended from horses that were brought to the continent by European settlers from the 1500s onwards. Many of these breeds had important roles to play – they are horses that carried pioneers over inhospitable mountains, took soldiers into battle during the Civil War and rounded up cattle on the Great Plains. Others, like the Appaloosa, were developed by North America's Indigenous peoples and reflect another side of the continent's story.

APPALOOSA
USA

BASHKIR CURLY
USA

PONY OF THE AMERICAS
USA

CAYUSE INDIAN PONY
USA

MISSOURI FOX TROTTER
USA

GALICEÑO
MEXICO

Bashkir Curlies may have originated with North America's Indigenous peoples. A Sioux artwork from 1801 shows horses with unusual curly coats among the tribe's ponies. They may have been bred to have thick coats, to help the horses survive in tough winter conditions.

Galiceños are one of the rarest breeds in the world. There are thought to only be a few hundred of these Mexican horses alive today.

CANADIAN HORSE — CANADA

AMERICAN SHETLAND — USA

MORGAN — USA

ROCKY MOUNTAIN HORSE — USA

QUARTER HORSE — USA

AMERICAN STANDARDBRED — USA

AMERICAN SADDLEBRED — USA

A horse called Beautiful Jim Key was a famous performer in America in the early 20th century. Described as the 'smartest horse in the world', Jim was said to be able to count, spell and tell the time.

INDIGENOUS PEOPLES AND HORSES

North America is probably the original home of the horse – it evolved there about 56 million years ago, then spread into Europe and Asia. But all horses in North America mysteriously died out about 10,000 years ago. Native Americans first encountered horses in the 16th century, when European colonisers (and their horses) arrived. At first, they were afraid of these animals as European settlers rode on horseback to capture villages. But as herds began to roam free, they were adopted by Indigenous peoples, helping them to hunt, travel, trade and protect their land from European invaders. Horses became an important part of Indigenous culture, celebrated in art and dances, and loved as companions.

NORTH AMERICA

CANADIAN HORSE

The Canadian Horse (or Cheval Canadien) is a rare and beautiful breed. All Canadian Horses can be traced back to a group of mares and stallions that were sent from France to eastern Canada between 1665 and 1670. These horses had been hand-picked from the royal stables of the king of France, Louis XIV, and they were probably a mix of Bretons (p53) and Norman Cobs (p50).

Once the horses set hoof in Canada, they were rented out to French settlers who were farming the mountainous landscape in what is now the province of Quebec. Over the next hundred years, the horses were bred in isolation, developing a unique look and personality.

These hardy horses were bred to cope with Canada's long, cold winters. Their strength and sturdiness made them ideal for pulling sleighs.

Straight ears · Wise expression · Short head · Graceful, arched neck · Broad, strong back · Long, heavy mane and tail

HORSE PROFILE
Country: Canada **Type:** Light
Height: 14–16.2 hands
Colours: Usually black, bay or brown, but can be any colour
Personality: Loyal, robust, intelligent

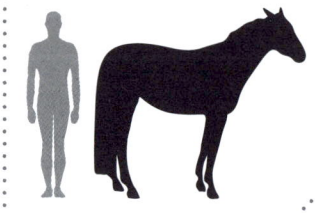

Nicknamed the 'little iron horse', this compact, strong breed was used for a range of jobs, such as pulling sleighs and stagecoaches, racing, farm work and carrying soldiers into battle during the American Civil War. In 2002, they were made an official symbol of Canada, which shows thier importance in the nation's history and culture.

MORGAN

The Morgan originated in the US state of Vermont in the 1790s and was one of the first breeds to be developed in America. All Morgans are descended from a stallion named Figure, who was owned by a man called Justin Morgan. Figure was a small horse, but was an exceptionally fast racer and hard worker. Figure was bred with local mares and passed on his strength, stamina and gentle nature to his foals.

In the 19th century, Morgans were seen as perfect all-purpose horses. They were used for riding and racing and as coach horses and as military mounts. Today, their quiet steadiness and affectionate characters make Morgans a popular choice for children and beginner riders, and excellent therapy horses.

HORSE PROFILE
Country: USA **Type:** Light
Height: 14.1–15.2 hands
Colours: Chestnut, bay, black or brown
Personality: Athletic, calm, strong

AMERICAN STANDARDBRED

The American Standardbred may sound ordinary, but it is actually pretty special. One of the fastest horses in the world, the breed was developed in the USA in the 1870s for a sport called harness racing.

During harness racing, shown here, a horse pulls a small, two-wheeled cart around a 1.6-km-long (1 mile) track as quick as it can – modern Standardbreds can zoom around a racecourse in under 2 minutes. As well as being speedy, Standardbreds are steady horses. Retired racers are often used in historical battle re-enactments in America due to their calm and dependable natures.

HORSE PROFILE
Country: USA
Type: Light **Height:** 15–16 hands
Colours: Bay, brown or chestnut
Personality: Steady, fast, friendly

The name Standardbred dates back to the breed's early development. Horses were only allowed to be registered as Standardbreds if they met a certain 'standard' of speed – they had to be able to trot 1.6 km (1 mile) in 2 minutes 30 seconds or less.

NORTH AMERICA

AMERICAN SHETLAND

Scottish Shetland ponies (p39) arrived in America in the 1880s and US breeders set about developing their own version of the much-loved miniature breed. They crossed Shetlands with Hackneys (p41), Welsh ponies (p42) and Arabs (p88) to create a pony that was taller and more elegant than its stocky cousins.

The most popular pony breed in the USA, American Shetlands are often used to pull small buggies in shows. This allows them to display their striking high-stepping trot, which they inherited from their Hackney ancestors.

Elegant head

Thick mane and tail (but doesn't have a thick coat like a Scottish Shetland)

Narrow body

Slender legs with dainty hooves

HORSE PROFILE
Country: USA
Type: Pony **Height:** 11.2 hands
Colours: All solid colours
Personality: Spirited, sweet, stylish

PONY OF THE AMERICAS

This beautiful breed is guaranteed to knock the spots off any other pony in the field. The Pony of the Americas was developed in Iowa in the 1950s when a Shetland stallion (p39) was bred with an Appaloosa mare (p22), producing a foal with a snow-white coat and black spots.

Quarter Horses (p20), Arabs (p88) and Welsh ponies (p42) were later added to create a sweet-natured pony that looks like a small horse and is tailor-made for children to ride and show. Unlike Shetlands, Ponies of the Americas have narrow backs, allowing kids to reach the stirrups easily and sit comfortably in the saddle.

Ponies of the Americas come in nine patterns. These include 'leopard', with spots all over the body, and 'blanket' with markings on the loin and hips.

Straight, narrow back

Visible whites of eyes (called sclera)

Spotty coat

Short, strong legs

Striped hooves

HORSE PROFILE
Country: USA **Type:** Pony
Height: 11.2–14 hands **Colours:** Typically black, brown or chestnut spots
Personality: Obedient, gentle, reliable

ROCKY MOUNTAIN HORSE

This nimble horse can trace its history to the 1890s, when a stallion was brought from the Rocky Mountains in the western United States to the Appalachian Mountains in the east and bred with local mares. The breed was properly developed in Kentucky from the 1960s onwards.

What makes the Rocky Mountain horse so special and so suited to its mountain home is its 'lateral gait'. This means that its feet hit the ground one at a time, allowing the horse to move smoothly over bumpy ground and keep its rider comfortable. As a result, these steady horses are popular for trail riding.

HORSE PROFILE
Country: USA
Type: Light **Height:** 14–16 hands
Colours: Usually chocolate with a flaxen mane, but can be any solid colour
Personality: Kind, sure-footed, trustworthy

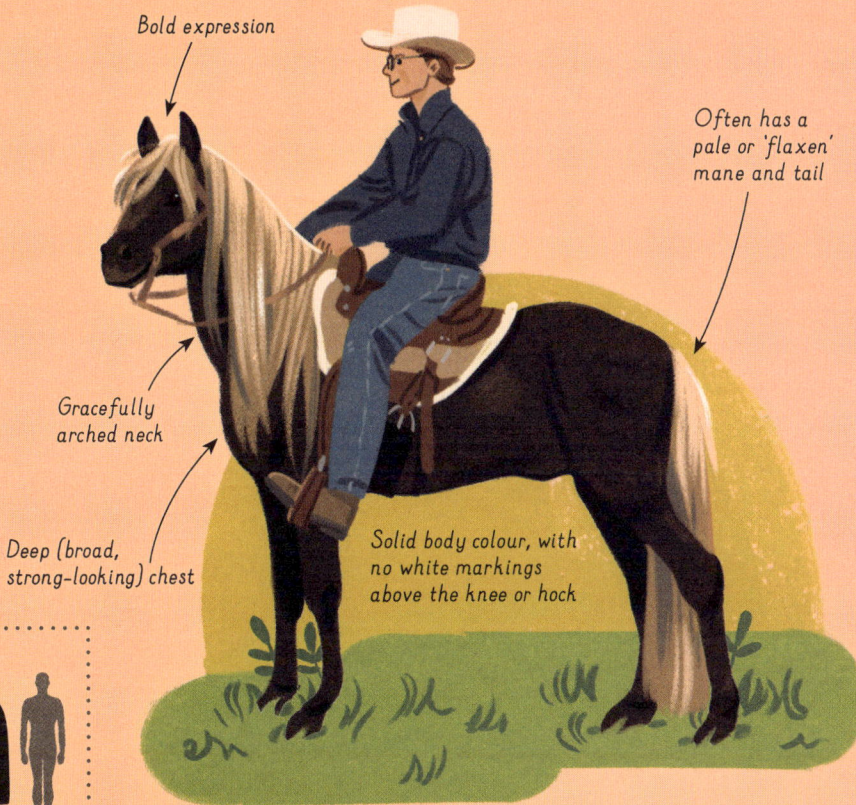

Bold expression
Often has a pale or 'flaxen' mane and tail
Gracefully arched neck
Deep (broad, strong-looking) chest
Solid body colour, with no white markings above the knee or hock

AMERICAN SADDLEBRED

Nicknamed 'the horse America made', this super-stylish breed was developed in Kentucky by crossing a now extinct horse called the Narragansett Pacer with Thoroughbreds (p41) and, later, Morgans (p17). The Pacer was prized for its smooth gait, which the Saddlebred has inherited.

The breed started out as a beautiful but practical farm horse, and many were used as military mounts in the American Civil War. Today, Saddlebreds are more commonly seen in the show ring where their combination of beauty, confidence and distinctive high-stepping trot make them the ultimate performers.

HORSE PROFILE
Country: USA
Type: Light **Height:** 15–16 hands
Colours: Any colour, including black, grey, chestnut, pinto or palomino
Personality: Elegant, athletic, versatile

Pointed ears set close together
Big, expressive eyes
Short, strong back
Long neck
Rounded ribs
Elegant legs

Saddlebreds can suffer from health problems caused by the exaggerated movements some horses are trained to perform in the show ring.

NORTH AMERICA

QUARTER HORSE

Saddle up and meet the Quarter Horse! A companion to cowboys and farmers, this all-American breed is one of the USA's oldest, and the nation's most popular horse. Quarter Horses were originally developed by European settlers in the 17th century to take part in quarter-mile races – short sprints that were held down the main streets of villages in eastern America. In the early 19th century, they found a new role as settlers started to move from the east of America to the west. These sturdy steeds were cooperative and fast on their feet, making them perfect for rounding up unruly cattle on North America's Great Plains.

Today, Quarter Horses are still prized for their 'cow sense' – their in-built ability to move and guide cattle. As well as working on ranches, they're also used for racing, cowboy contests known as rodeos and trail riding.

Short, wide head
Intelligent expression
Deep chest
Compact body
Strong hindquarters

HORSE PROFILE
Country: USA
Type: Light **Height:** 15–15.3 hands
Colours: Any solid colour, though the most popular is chestnut
Personality: Fast, friendly, hard-working

Quarter Horses really are fast. Some have been recorded running up to 88.5 km (55 miles) per hour!

MISSOURI FOX TROTTER

This graceful horse comes from the Ozark Mountains in Missouri and Arkansas. In the early 19th century, the local people needed horses that could work hard on their farms but also carry them comfortably over tough terrain. They bred sure-footed and strong horses together, including Morgans (p17), Thoroughbreds (p41) and, later, American Saddlebreds (p19), to create this adaptable breed.

The breed is partly named after its unusual way of walking – it moves a front foot just before it moves the opposite back foot. This means its back remains very steady, making it super smooth to ride over even the rockiest of mountains.

HORSE PROFILE
Country: USA
Type: Light **Height:** 14–16 hands
Colours: Any colour, including chestnut, palomino, grey or champagne
Personality: Strong, agile, elegant

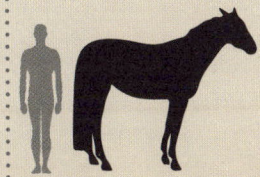

Alert, pointed ears
Sloped, strong shoulders
Broad back
Muscular body
Deep chest
Tough feet

BASHKIR CURLY

In 1898, John Damele and his son, Peter, were riding in the mountains of Nevada when they saw something unusual in a herd of Mustang (p56) – three of the wild horses had thick, curly coats. The Dameles tamed the curly horses and bred them with Arabs (p88) and Morgans (p17) to create this wonderfully woolly breed.

Their curls are the result of a special gene that has been passed down from the original Mustangs. Curlies are tough – their coats get extra-thick in winter to protect them from the cold – but they also have gentle characters to match their lamb-like looks.

Curly coat, which is thick in winter and thinner in summer
Low withers
Short back
Very thick, wavy or curly tail and mane
Curly eyelashes
Short, strong legs

HORSE PROFILE
Country: USA
Type: Light **Height:** 15 hands
Colours: Any colour, though often chestnut, grey, bay or black
Personality: Intelligent, calm, hardy

NORTH AMERICA

CAYUSE INDIAN PONY

This extremely rare breed takes its name from the Cayuse, an Indigenous group who originally lived in the valleys and mountains of Northwest America. The Cayuse, such as the rider shown here in traditional dress, were known for their incredible horse skills. They used their horses to hunt bison, fight, trade and travel.

Cayuse Indian Ponies are thought to have descended from Percherons (p50) that were brought to America from Canada by French settlers. The Cayuse possibly crossed these powerful horses with lighter, Spanish breeds to create their small, strong ponies. Said to be capable of carrying their riders from dawn to dusk without stopping, the endurance of Cayuse Indian Ponies was the stuff of legend.

Only a small number of these special horses are thought to survive in California and Kentucky, where fans are trying to build a herd and protect them from extinction.

Sloped pasterns give the pony a broken walking gait, which makes it comfortable to ride.

HORSE PROFILE
Country: USA
Type: Pony **Height:** 14 hands
Colours: Any colour **Personality:** Brave, fast, strong

APPALOOSA

If you want a horse that stands out from the crowd, you've turned to the right page. The stunning Appaloosa is thought to have descended from Spanish horses brought to North America in the 17th century and adopted by the Indigenous Nez Perce people. The Nez Perce were skilled horse breeders, who picked only the strongest, fastest and hardiest horses.

Appaloosa horses almost became extinct in the 1870s, when the US government stole Nez Perce land. Admirers saved the breed in the 1930s and today these beautiful and one-of-a-kind horses are used for riding, racing and jumping all over the world.

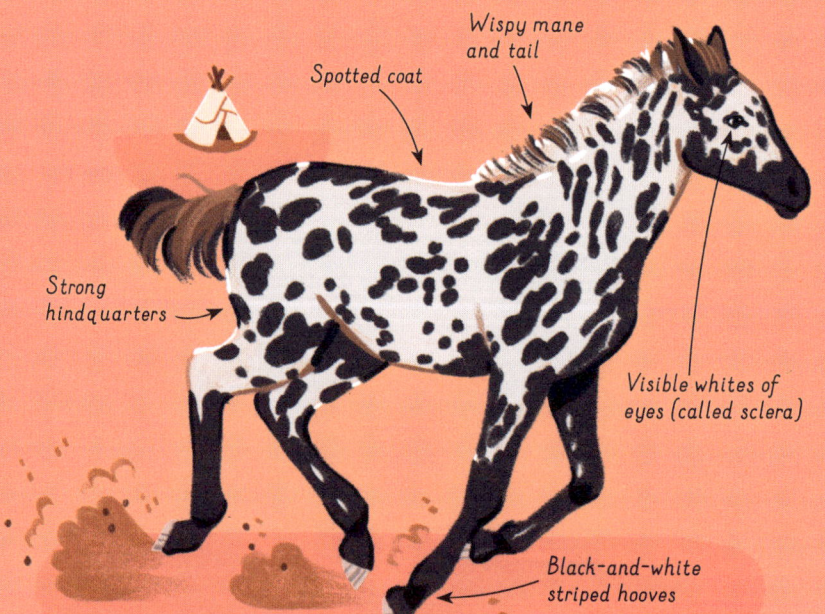

HORSE PROFILE
Country: USA
Type: Light **Height:** 14.2–15.2 hands
Colours: Various spotty patterns
Personality: Biddable, hardy, loyal

It's thought the name Appaloosa comes from the Palouse River, which runs through the land of the Nez Perce people. Over time 'Palouse' became 'Appaloosa'.

GALICEÑO

Tiny but tough sums up this rare Mexican breed. The Galiceño (you say it 'gal-eh-seen-yo') is descended from Spanish and Portuguese horses brought to the Americas by European settlers in the 16th century. These little horses had to be extra hardy to survive the voyage across the Atlantic Ocean, and when they reached Mexico, many were used for work in mines and on farms. Others were left to roam free and were adopted by local people.

Over the centuries, the horses developed naturally in Mexico before catching the attention of breeders in America in the 1950s. Many were then imported to the USA, and the Galiceño became an official breed in 1958.

Despite being the size of a pony, Galiceños have horse-like proportions and kindly natures, making them a great choice for young riders. These sturdy steeds are perfectly capable of carrying adults, too. Their strength and inquisitiveness mean Galiceños are happy to try their hoof at all sorts of activities, from dressage and jumping to pulling carts and cattle driving.

Small, alert ears
Narrow head
Short back
Fine, silky mane and tail
Deep, narrow chest
Strong legs with small, hard feet

The breed's name comes from an area of Spain called Galicia, reflecting its European roots.

HORSE PROFILE
Country: Mexico
Type: Pony **Height:** 12–13.2 hands
Colours: Any solid colours, often black, bay or chestnut
Personality: Friendly, hardy, curious

FABULOUS FOALS

There's nothing cuter than a tiny foal taking its first frolic in a field. But baby horses don't stay little for long. A lot goes on in the first year of a horse's life and there are important milestones each foal should experience so it can grow into a healthy and happy adult. Let's follow one foal for a year and see what she gets up to.

Just born

Meet Willow. This little foal has just been born. Her mother licks Willow to warm her up and establish their bond. Within an hour, Willow has stood up, taken her first wobbly steps and had her first drink of milk from her mum. This first milk is filled with nutrients that will help Willow grow, as well as antibodies that will protect her from infection.

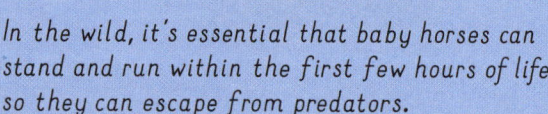

In the wild, it's essential that baby horses can stand and run within the first few hours of life so they can escape from predators.

Heading outdoors: 1 week old

Willow spends at least a third of her day snoozing and will suckle milk from her mum two or three times an hour. Willow and her mum are let out of their stable each day to enjoy some gentle exercise. The little foal stays close to her mum, but might try a short canter if she's feeling confident! Willow's human owners gently stroke her, so she gets used to being handled by people.

Trying new things: 2-4 weeks

By now, Willow will have had her first taste of solid food, taking a nibble of her mum's hay – mmm, grassy! She will also play with her mum to develop social skills. When she is about 4 weeks old she will be seen by a horse foot expert (known as a farrier), who will check that her hooves are developing properly and give Willow her first gentle trim.

Young foals sometimes eat their mum's poop! Although this sounds gross, it's thought this helps the foal to develop healthy gut bacteria.

Independent Willow: 4-7 months

Willow is becoming more independent and developing grown-up-horse behaviours. She'll spend less time playing and more time grazing, for example. Willow is still drinking her mum's milk, but she is getting most of her nutrients from grass and feed. At 6 months, Willow will be given her first vaccinations by a vet to protect her from horse diseases.

Weaning: 8-12 months

Willow now gets her nutrients from solid food and will gradually stop drinking mum's milk – a process known as weaning. Willow's owners encourage her to spend more time with other horses and less time with her mum. They also introduce some basic training, such as walking on a lead, being groomed and wearing a horse blanket.

Making friends: 2-3 months

Willow is becoming much more confident and spends more time playing with other foals in the field – it's so much fun, she can't help jumping and bucking with excitement! Playtime helps Willow to develop social bonds and learn boundaries. Willow and her friends may also groom one another to strengthen their relationships.

Happy birthday, Willow!: 1 year old

Willow is now a 'yearling'. Her owners continue gentle training so she will become comfortable around humans. She'll also spend lots of time with other yearlings in the field to help her develop into a happy, confident young horse. She'll continue to grow through her 'teenage years' and become an adult when she is around 4–5 years old.

SOUTH AMERICA

All horses in South America are descended from stallions and mares that were brought to the continent by Europeans in the 16th century. In the centuries since, these horses have undergone incredible transformations that have resulted in stylish, spirited breeds. In this chapter, we'll meet ponies left to roam wild in the deep forests of Brazil, equines that carry Argentine cowboys (gauchos) across endless plains, and Peruvian horses with one-of-a-kind footwork. Get ready for an epic ride!

Modern horses were introduced to South America by Spanish invaders, called conquistadors, from the 1530s, like the one shown here. These soldiers used their horses to travel across the continent and take control of Indigenous lands and empires by force. The conquistadors' horses included Barbs (p76) and Andalusians (p60).

CAMPOLINA
BRAZIL

MANGALARGA MARCHADOR
BRAZIL

PASO FINO
COLOMBIA

PERUVIAN PASO
PERU

A LAND OF HORSES

Horses were prized by the conquistadors, but many were lost or abandoned as the soldiers made their way across the continent. These horses eventually found a new home with South America's Indigenous peoples.

The Tehuelche, for example, were a group of people in Patagonia – a region of enormous mountains and grasslands at the southern tip of South America. By the 18th century, horses had become an essential part of their lives and culture. Horses helped the Tehuelche to navigate the difficult landscape more easily, allowing them to hunt, travel and trade with other Indigenous groups in the north.

A Tehuelche rider

PAMPA HORSE BRAZIL

CAMPEIRO BRAZIL

ARGENTINE CRIOLLO ARGENTINA

The Argentine Criollo is renowned for its stamina. Each year, breeders take part in an endurance race called La Marcha, which covers 750 km (466 miles) over 2 weeks, to show off their horses' long-distance skills.

ARGENTINE POLO PONY ARGENTINA

CHILEAN HORSE CHILE

FALABELLA ARGENTINA

Although they have much smaller bodies than regular horses, Falabellas have hearts that are as big as a larger horse. It's thought this helps give them a particularly long lifespan – Falabellas typically live for between 40 and 45 years.

SOUTH AMERICA

PERUVIAN PASO

You can recognise this horse by the way it moves. The Peruvian Paso has an incredibly smooth and special way of walking – it has a slow, even gait, known as *paso llano*. During *paso llano* the horse may also swing its front legs outwards, creating a gentle rolling movement (called *termino*).

These signature moves had a practical purpose. The Peruvian Paso is descended from Spanish horses brought to South America by conquistadors in the 16th century. They were used to carry riders over Peru's harsh deserts and mountains, and to work on vast ranches. As well as being hardy and easy to handle, they had to have a smooth gait so a rider could sit in the saddle for a long time without bouncing around.

Because they are so comfortable to ride, Peruvian Pasos make excellent trail horses. They are also sought after by riders with hip or back pain. In fact, this horse is so steady, it's said that you can hold a glass of water while riding a Peruvian Paso and never spill a drop!

- Short, muscular neck
- Broad back
- Confident, proud expression
- Flexible joints
- Termino movement
- Glossy mane and tail
- Long, powerful hind legs

HORSE PROFILE
Country: Peru
Type: Light **Height:** 14.1–15.2 hands
Colours: Any colour, including chestnut, bay, black, palomino or grey
Personality: Friendly, confident, stylish

Breeders of Peruvian Pasos look for horses with brio. Horses that have brio have a natural confidence and controlled energy, without being fiery or hard to handle.

PASO FINO

The beautiful Paso Fino is descended from Spanish horses, including Andalusians (p60) and an extinct breed called the Jennet, which were brought to the Caribbean and Central and South America by Europeans. Two versions of the breed developed in Colombia and Puerto Rico, and today, the Colombian Paso Fino is the more widespread.

Like the Peruvian Paso (see opposite), the Paso Fino has a natural lateral gait, which makes the horse extremely comfortable to ride – *paso fino* means 'fine step' in Spanish. Originally used to carry landowners around their vast plantations, these sure-footed horses are now used for a variety of activities, including trail riding, endurance competitions and parades.

Luxurious mane and tail
Strong back
Gracefully arched neck
A fairly small horse but powerful for its size
Straight, strong legs

HORSE PROFILE
Country: Colombia and Puerto Rico
Type: Light **Height:** 13–15.2 hands
Colours: Any colour
Personality: Sensible, people-orientated, athletic

The Paso Fino has a four-beat lateral gait which is performed at three different speeds – classic fino (slow), paso corto (moderate speed) and paso largo (fast).

CHILEAN HORSE

The national horse of Chile, these horses have been the companions of the country's *huasos* (skilled horseback riders) for centuries and are South America's oldest registered breed. They are descended from Spanish horses that were imported to Chile from Peru in the 16th century, and then developed in the country in isolation.

As a result, they are perfectly adapted to the extreme landscapes of their home nation. Bred to control cattle in Chile's towering mountains and windswept plains, Chilean Horses are tough, agile and not easily spooked. They are still used to work cattle and for rodeos and are a great choice for mountain trail riding.

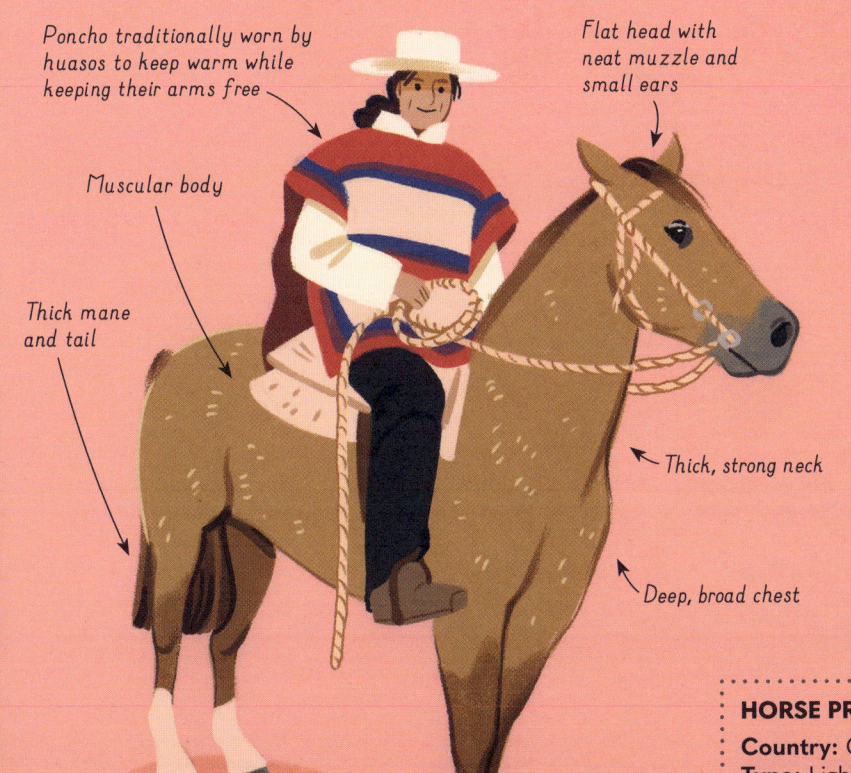

Poncho traditionally worn by huasos to keep warm while keeping their arms free
Flat head with neat muzzle and small ears
Muscular body
Thick mane and tail
Thick, strong neck
Deep, broad chest

HORSE PROFILE
Country: Chile
Type: Light **Height:** Around 14.3 hands
Colours: Any colour, though black or chestnut are common
Personality: Intelligent, strong, good-natured

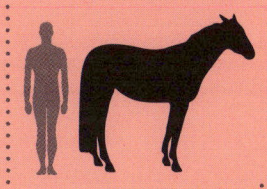

SOUTH AMERICA

Two Argentine Criollos named Gato and Mancha took part in an epic ride from Buenos Aires in Argentina to New York in the USA between 1925 and 1928 – a distance of over 16,000 km (10,000 miles).

Intelligent expression
Long muzzle
Strong, sloping shoulders
Broad chest
Compact, muscly body

ARGENTINE CRIOLLO

Not many horses have the skill to trek across the mountains of Patagonia, or the stamina to race for hours through the grasslands of the Pampas . . . except the Argentine Criollo. These horses are brave, tough and free-spirited, just like the legendary *gauchos* (Argentine cowboys) who ride them, such as the rider in this image, shown wearing traditional dress.

Criollos are descended from a group of Spanish horses that were brought to Argentina in the 1530s by European explorers and left to fend for themselves. The offspring of these horses were later recaptured and tamed by Spanish settlers and local people. In the time they'd been wild, the horses had become perfectly adapted to Argentina's extreme climate. A Criollo can work through hot summers and bitterly cold winters, survive on little food and water, is resistant to many common horse diseases and lives for at least 30 years.

HORSE PROFILE
Country: Argentina
Type: Light **Height:** 14–15 hands
Colours: Any colour, except paint
Personality: Strong, independent, hard-working

Criollos were used to carry riders over tricky terrain to round up cattle and tend to land. They are still used as cattle horses, as well as for trail riding and rodeos. Because of their incredible endurance, they have been used for long-distance journeys and races.

30

ARGENTINE POLO PONY

These lightning-quick horses are bred to play a sport called polo, where teams on horseback use a long mallet to hit a ball through a goal (a bit like playing hockey on a horse).

When the sport arrived in South America in the late 19th century, Argentinian breeders decided to create their own polo pony. They combined the stamina and toughness of the Criollo (see opposite) with the swiftness of the Thoroughbred (p41) to create a breed that can twist and turn in a split second and has an instinctive talent for the game. Despite having 'Pony' in their name, this is a light horse breed.

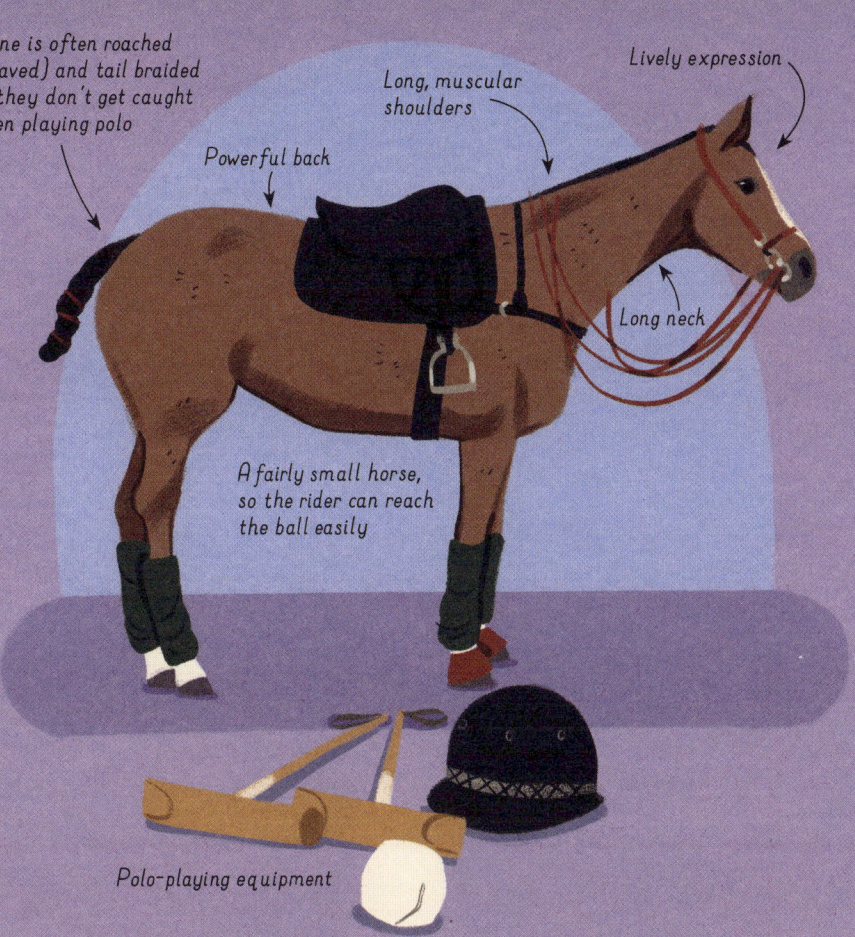

Mane is often roached (shaved) and tail braided so they don't get caught when playing polo

Long, muscular shoulders

Lively expression

Powerful back

Long neck

A fairly small horse, so the rider can reach the ball easily

Polo-playing equipment

HORSE PROFILE
Country: Argentina **Type:** Light
Height: 14.2–15 hands
Colours: Any colour but often bay
Personality: Fast, agile, bold

FALABELLA

Meet one of the smallest horses in the world. Falabellas are descended from Spanish horses brought to Argentina in the 16th century then left to roam free on the Pampas (grassy plains). Centuries of wandering long distances to find food, and coping with high winds and hot summers, created horses that were small, strong and spirited. Many were adopted by the Indigenous Mapuche people, who sold a herd to horse breeders in the 19th century – the modern Falabella is descended from this herd. Shetland Ponies (p39), small Thoroughbreds (p41) and Criollos (p30) were used to perfect the breed.

Today's Falabellas make sweet pets, who love to be around people. Thanks to their portable size, they can access places that regular-sized horses can't – such as schools and care homes – and are often used as therapy and even guide horses.

Intelligent, kindly expression

Thick, silky manes

Sturdy, oval hooves

Compact body

HORSE PROFILE
Country: Argentina
Type: Pony **Height:** 8 hands
Colours: All colours, including spotted
Personality: Clever, friendly, gentle

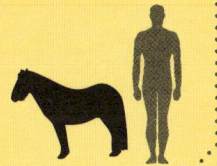

31

SOUTH AMERICA

MANGALARGA MARCHADOR

The national horse of Brazil, this breed has its origins in the late 18th century, when a Portuguese stallion called Sublime was brought to the country and bred with Spanish Jennets and Andalusians (p60). The Jennet was renowned for its smooth gait, which it passed on to the Marchador.

Although these horses look proud, they don't mind getting their hooves muddy. They are often seen helping farmers herd cattle on Brazilian ranches, as well as being used in sports such as polo, cross-country racing and showjumping.

HORSE PROFILE
Country: Brazil
Type: Light **Height:** 14.2–16 hands
Colours: All colours, including grey, chestnut, black, palomino or paint
Personality: Sensible, agile, gentle

CAMPOLINA

With its majestic body and exaggerated nose, the Campolina has a horsey style all of its own. These unusual-looking horses are named after a farmer, Cassiano Campolina, who developed them in the 1870s. He crossed a Barb mare (p76) with an Andalusian stallion (p60), and their colt became the founding horse of the breed. Clydesdales (p38) were later introduced for strength, and Holsteiners (p54) and Marchadors (see above) for flair and elegance.

Campolinas are typically used for leisure riding and make particularly comfortable rides on long-distance trails thanks to their smooth gait. They are also a popular choice for dressage in Brazil.

HORSE PROFILE
Country: Brazil
Type: Light **Height:** 15–15.2 hands
Colours: Any colour, but silver-grey is very popular
Personality: Good-tempered, confident, graceful

Brazil is home to around 85,000 of these striking horses.

CAMPEIRO

In the south of Brazil, a dense forest of pine trees once stretched for hundreds of square kilometres over mountains and plateaus. Here in the 16th century, a group of Spanish explorers lost some of their horses. Left to roam among the spiky trees for hundreds of years, the descendants of these mares and stallions became small, tough and used to thinking for themselves.

From the 1700s onwards, many of these horses were tamed, selectively bred for their natural ambling gait, and developed into the breed known today as the Campeiro. Often used for leisure riding and for pulling light loads, Campeiros also make good cattle horses due to their independence and intelligence.

Alert ears
Small, compact body
Lively expression
Delicate neck
Strong, slender legs

HORSE PROFILE
Country: Brazil
Type: Light **Height:** 14.1–15.1 hands
Colours: Any colour, but most common are chestnut, bay or grey
Personality: Clever, friendly, agile

PAMPA HORSE

The Pampa Horse is Brazil's spotted (or pinto) breed. Its origins are unclear – it's thought the breed developed from horses brought to Brazil by European settlers in the 16th century, and refined with other South American horses, such as the Marchador (see opposite) and the Criollo (p30).

The Pampa Horse's most obvious feature is its spectacular coat, which is a dazzling white with black- or brown-coloured patches. They have a natural gait, making them very easy to ride. As well as being used for leisure riding, these multi-talented horses can be seen working on Brazilian farms and taking part in long-distance treks.

Intelligent expression
Silky mane and tail
Muscular body
Spotted, or pinto, coat
Strong legs
Round, tough hooves

HORSE PROFILE
Country: Brazil
Type: Light **Height:** 14–14.2 hands
Colours: Pinto pattern of white and dark colours
Personality: Energetic, good-natured, adaptable

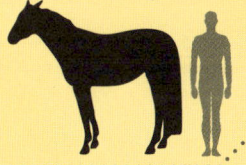

DONKEYS, MULES AND HINNIES

Compared to a dazzling palomino or a dashing Thoroughbred, a little grey donkey looks pretty ordinary. But donkeys and their relatives – mules and hinnies – are extraordinary equines. With around 60 million donkeys and mules in the world today, and over 180 donkey breeds, these intelligent, gentle and hard-working animals deserve to be celebrated.

DONKEY WORLD

Donkeys have lived and worked alongside us for at least 6,000 years. They are descended from African wild asses (p80) that were first tamed in northeast Africa, before being brought to Europe and Asia. These humble animals transformed human lives during ancient times, helping farmers to plough fields, and carrying people and goods over long distances.

Because their wild ancestors lived in deserts and savannas, donkeys can survive in difficult conditions. As well as being tough, they are amazingly strong. Millions of donkeys are still used to carry loads and work the land, especially in Africa and Asia.

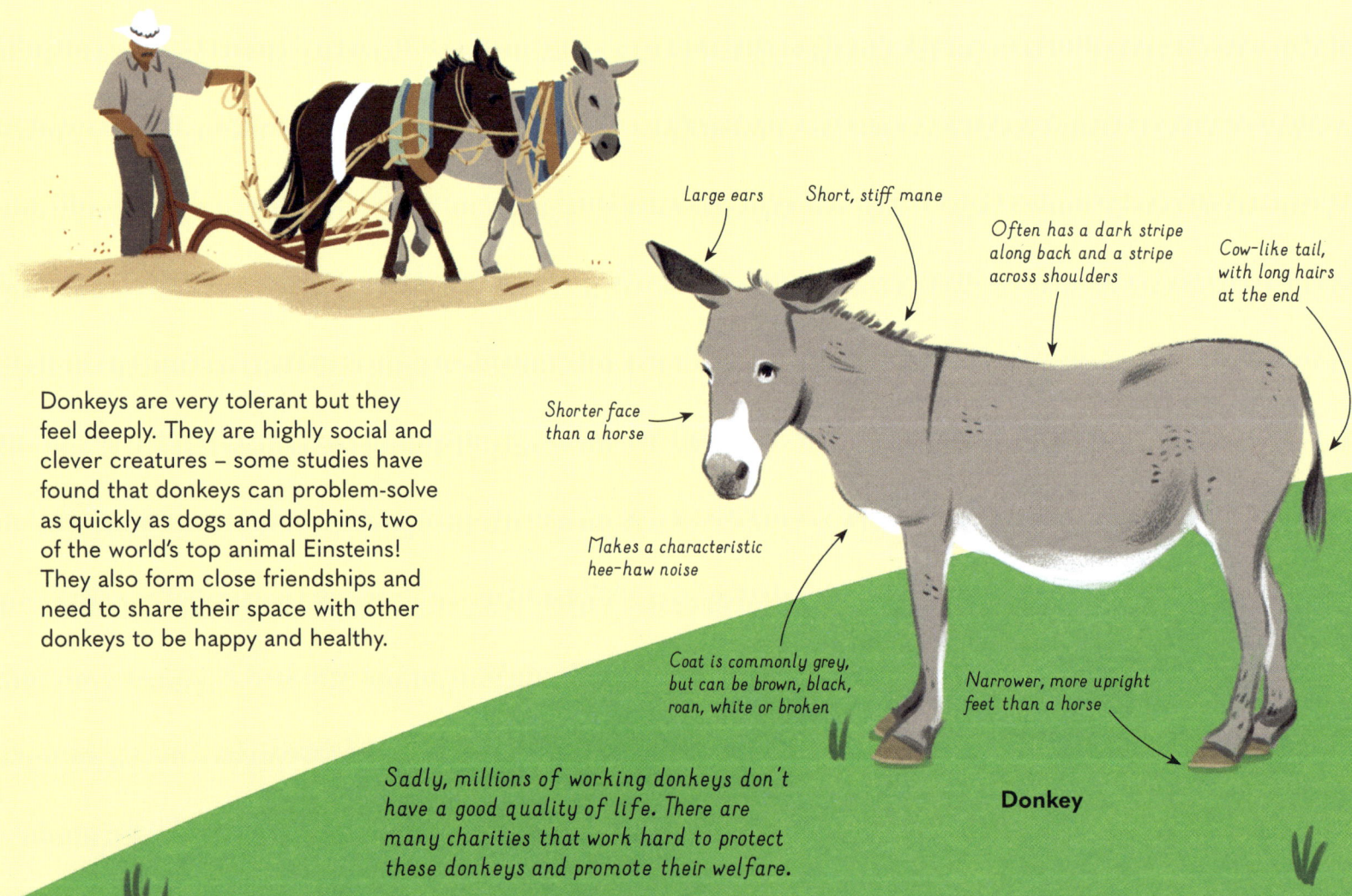

Donkeys are very tolerant but they feel deeply. They are highly social and clever creatures – some studies have found that donkeys can problem-solve as quickly as dogs and dolphins, two of the world's top animal Einsteins! They also form close friendships and need to share their space with other donkeys to be happy and healthy.

Sadly, millions of working donkeys don't have a good quality of life. There are many charities that work hard to protect these donkeys and promote their welfare.

Labels on donkey:
- Large ears
- Short, stiff mane
- Often has a dark stripe along back and a stripe across shoulders
- Cow-like tail, with long hairs at the end
- Shorter face than a horse
- Makes a characteristic hee-haw noise
- Coat is commonly grey, but can be brown, black, roan, white or broken
- Narrower, more upright feet than a horse

Donkey

MULES RULE!

Because horses and donkeys are closely related, they can breed with one another and have young that are known as hybrids. A mule is the hybrid offspring of a male donkey and a female horse. A hinny is the result of a male horse breeding with a female donkey.

How can you tell if you're petting a mule or a hinny? A mule has the head of a donkey and the body of a horse, while a hinny has a horse-like head and a donkey body. Hinnies tend to be more horsey in their behaviour too, whereas mules take after their donkey parent.

Like donkeys, mules and hinnies have been used for thousands of years to carry loads and help with farm work. Mules can pull even heavier loads than donkeys. These tough animals are known for being strong-minded, but their stubbornness is actually a reflection of their intelligence – mules like to think before they do something, making them much safer to ride over tough terrain than horses.

Long ears and donkey-like head

Thin tail and mane

Strong, horse-like body

Short ears

Horse-like head

Usually has a donkey-like body

Longer mane and tail compared to a mule

Both mules and hinnies make a noise that's half donkey hee-haw, half horsey whinny.

Long, thin legs

Tough hooves

Mule

Hinny

Mules and hinnies have a trait called hybrid vigour. This is when a crossbreed animal is stronger and healthier than its parents. Mules and hinnies are often very resistant to common horse and donkey illnesses, for example.

EUROPE (North & West)

Northern and Western Europe are the birthplace of some of the world's oldest and best-loved breeds. This is the home of horsey heavyweights, such as the Shire and Percheron, nimble-hoofed athletes, such as the Thoroughbred and Holsteiner, and plucky ponies, like the Shetland and Welsh Mountain. As well as being bred for special roles, many of these horses were developed to thrive in certain environments — from Norwegian fjords and Austrian mountains to rolling English hills and Finnish pine forests.

Shires are still sometimes used by farmers as an environmentally friendly alternative to tractors. In London, UK, teams of Shires are used to plough and reseed meadows in the city's parks.

Some historians believe England's first Norman king, William the Conqueror, rode a Friesian at the Battle of Hastings in 1066.

EUROPE (North & West)

CLYDESDALE

Scotland's heavy horse gets its name from the rolling countryside that surrounds the River Clyde. The handsome and hardworking Clydesdale has its origins in the early 18th century, when stallions from Belgium and the Netherlands were brought to the area and bred with local mares. Another giant breed, the Shire (p40), was later added to the mix.

A Clydesdale's original job was to pull heavy farm equipment, but the breed's strength, stamina and obedient nature saw these horses being put to use in all manner of ways – from hauling coal and milk wagons to pulling trams in towns. Their saucepan-sized hooves meant Clydesdales were particularly suited to long days trudging through hard city streets, and they were a familiar sight in urban areas into the 20th century.

Wide forehead with white blaze

Sloped shoulders

Long legs with a characteristic high-stepping trot

Flowing, silky hairs (called feathers) on lower legs

Strong, muscular body

Enormous hooves

By the 1950s, Clydesdales had been largely replaced on farms and roads by tractors and trucks, and the breed was at risk of extinction. They are still a rare breed today, but if you're lucky, you can see these magnificent horses strutting their stuff in parades or country shows.

HORSE PROFILE
Country: Scotland, UK
Type: Heavy **Height:** 16.2–18 hands
Colours: Bay, brown or black with white markings
Personality: Gentle, sensible, strong

SHETLAND PONY

The rugged Shetland Islands off the north coast of Scotland have been home to small ponies since the Bronze Age (around 4,000 years ago). The modern Shetland was developed in isolation there. They were bred to be incredibly tough, both to survive the islands' harsh climate and to perform difficult jobs. They were originally used to lug carts of seaweed and peat (a soil-like material used as fuel). During the 19th century, they were also taken to the mainland to work in coal mines.

Beneath their shaggy manes, Shetlands' black eyes glitter with determination – this is a clever breed with a spirit to match its strength. Although they have a stubborn side, Shetlands are gentle animals and their small size and sturdiness makes them popular riding ponies for young children.

Thick mane and tail to protect the pony from the cold
Small, alert ears
Intelligent expression
Powerful body
Short, strong legs with tough feet
Grows a double coat in winter

HORSE PROFILE
Country: Scotland, UK
Type: Pony **Height:** 10.2 hands
Colours: Any colour/pattern, except spotted
Personality: Intelligent, active, strong-willed

HIGHLAND

The earliest record of ponies in the Scottish Highlands dates back to 800 BCE, when a group of people called the Picts carved images of their horses on to stones. The Highland looks similar to these ancient horses. However, French and Spanish horses, Arabs (p88) and Clydesdales (see opposite) have been used over the last 500 years to refine the breed.

Perfectly adapted to the moors and mountains of Scotland's highlands and islands, these powerful, all-weather ponies were built for a life hauling timber through forests or carrying hunting equipment up hills. Prized for their calm nature, Highlands make an excellent choice for first-time or nervous riders.

Strong neck
Compact body
Long, silky mane
Kind expression
Wide hooves for walking on boggy and rocky ground

HORSE PROFILE
Country: Scotland, UK
Type: Pony **Height:** 13–14.2 hands
Colours: Various shades of dun, as well as grey, brown, black, bay or chestnut
Personality: Hardy, calm, adaptable

EUROPE (North & West)

SHIRE

Standing up to 19 hands high, the Shire is the world's tallest horse. This gentle giant is named after the counties ('shires') in England where it was developed in the 18th century, but its history goes back much further. The Shire is descended from the English Great Horse, an enormous breed that was ridden by medieval knights. To carry a knight in armour, with a combined weight of 180 kg (400 lbs), these horses had to be incredibly strong, as well as brave, to cope with the chaos of battle.

In the 16th century, Great Horses found a new role pulling ploughs on farms. Over the next 200 years, they were mixed with Belgian and Dutch breeds to create the Shire. By the 19th century, they had become part of everyday life in Britain. Millions were used to pull wagons in cities, carry cargo from docks and tow barges along canals, as shown below. However, their numbers declined from the 1950s, when advances in technology meant the horses were no longer needed for many of their jobs.

Arched neck
Short back
Expressive, gentle eyes
Muscly, powerful body
Stocky legs with thick feathering around feet
Very wide, dinner-plate-sized hooves
Often have white markings on face and legs

With fewer than 3,000 alive today, these magnificent horses are a rare but unmistakable sight.

HORSE PROFILE
Country: England
Type: Heavy **Height:** 17–19 hands
Colours: Black, brown, bay or grey
Personality: Loyal, hard-working, kindly

THOROUGHBRED

The king of the racetrack, the Thoroughbred was born to run. These speed machines have their origins in the 17th and 18th centuries, when horse racing became a popular hobby among English aristocrats. Wealthy stable owners bred fast English horses with Arabs (p88), Barbs (p76) and Turkish breeds to develop unbeatable horsey athletes.

Thoroughbreds can hit a top speed of 64–70 km (40–44 miles) per hour thanks to their streamlined bodies, long strides and powerful back legs, which propel them around a racecourse. Retired Thoroughbreds can be used for general riding but they need a very experienced owner – because their whole life is geared towards racing, they can be restless and easily spooked.

HORSE PROFILE
Country: England **Type:** Light
Height: 15–17 hands
Colours: Usually bay, chestnut, brown, black or grey
Personality: Athletic, spirited, bold

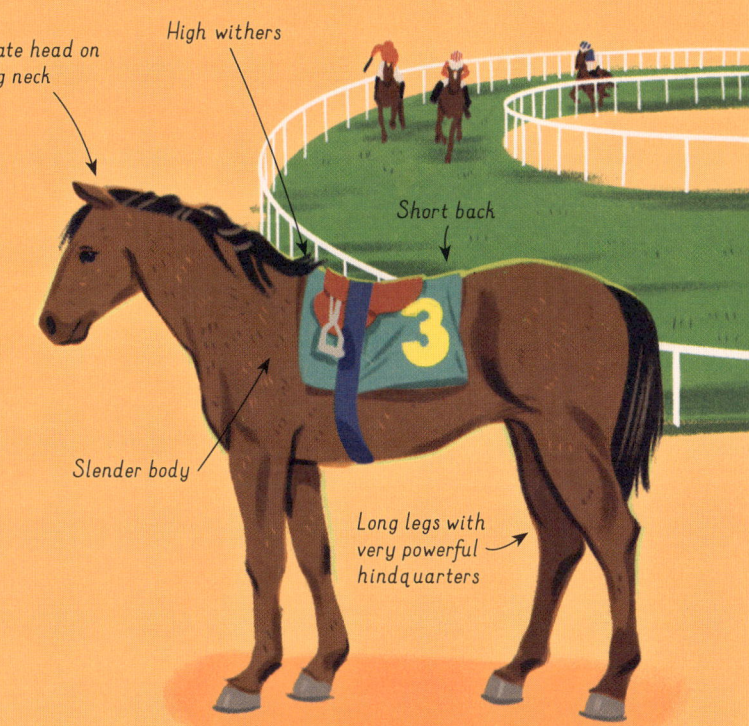

Delicate head on a long neck
High withers
Short back
Slender body
Long legs with very powerful hindquarters

Horse racing pushes horses to their physical limits. It comes with the risk of injury and can lead to health problems for Thoroughbreds.

HACKNEY

The Hackney is a stunning horse that combines strength with style. It originated in the 18th and 19th centuries when roads improved and there was an increased demand for horses to pull carriages, as shown on the left. Hackneys were perfect for the job because they could cover a lot of ground quickly – in 1800, a Hackney mare called Phenomena was recorded trotting 27 km (17 miles) in 53 minutes.

Hackneys were also a status symbol, with their snappy, high-stepping trot setting them apart from the average horse on the road. Hackneys are rare nowadays, but you can still see them demonstrating their nimble step and carriage skills in the show ring.

Head held upright and proudly
Powerful, sloping shoulders
Alert expression
Glossy coat
Very strong hocks (joints in back legs)
Round, neat hooves

HORSE PROFILE
Country: England
Type: Light **Height:** 14.2–16.2 hands
Colours: Any solid colour, including brown, chestnut, bay and black
Personality: Elegant, active, alert

EUROPE (North & West)

WELSH PONIES AND COBS

The wild hills of Wales are the birthplace of four much-loved breeds. Because they are so closely related, Welsh breeds are grouped into 'sections' based on height: the Welsh Mountain Pony (Section A), Welsh Pony (Section B), Welsh Pony of Cob Type (Section C), and Welsh Cob (Section D).

The Welsh Mountain Pony is the smallest and the breed from which the three others developed. This pretty pony can trace its history to small Celtic horses, which were brought to Wales during the Bronze Age (around 4,000 years ago). The modern breed was refined in the 18th century, when tough Welsh mares were crossed with dainty Thoroughbred (p41) and Arab (p88) stallions. Sure-footed, friendly and not easily spooked, they make outstanding ponies for children.

- Neat ears
- Small head, with a gentle dip between the eyes and nose (called a dished head)
- Bold expression
- Strong, well laid-back shoulders
- Muscular body and legs
- Dense hooves with silky feathering

Welsh Cob

- Short, strong back
- Silky mane and tail
- Elegant legs
- Big eyes with long lashes

Welsh Mountain Pony

The Welsh Cob is the largest Welsh breed and was developed to work on hilltop farms. Its compact size, courage and strength meant it was often used in coal mines in the 19th century and to carry soldiers and pull heavy guns during wars. Today, they excel in many sports, including dressage and driving.

HORSE PROFILE
Country: Wales **Types:** Pony and Light
Height: 12 hands (Section A), 12–13.2 hands (Sections B and C), over 13.2 hands (Section D)
Colours: Any colour except piebald or skewbald
Personality: Hardy, spirited, people-loving

IRISH DRAUGHT

The Irish Draught is the national horse of Ireland. It has its origins in war horses that were brought from France and Belgium in the 12th century and crossed with a now-extinct breed called the Irish Hobby.

The breed is lighter than the 'draught' part of its name suggests (as in pulling a heavy load). They were developed over centuries to be all-purpose farm workers – strong enough to pull a plough, agile enough to be ridden across the countryside, and stylish enough to take a cart into town.

Gentle expression · *Well-defined withers* · *Powerful back* · *Long, sloping croup (rump)* · *Graceful neck that holds head proudly* · *Muscular legs*

HORSE PROFILE
Country: Ireland **Type:** Light
Height: 15.2–16.3 hands
Colours: Any solid colour, including grey, bay, brown, black or dun
Personality: Adaptable, strong, sensible

Irish Draughts are excellent jumpers and are often bred with Thoroughbreds (p41) to create Irish Sport Horses, which are especially good at showjumping and dressage.

CONNEMARA

Connemara in the west of Ireland is a land of lonely mountains and craggy moors. The exact origins of the breed are unclear. One theory is that the ancestors of today's Connemara ponies may have been brought to Ireland by the Vikings. Over centuries, the ponies became perfectly adapted to their windswept home. When Spanish warships were wrecked on the coast in the 1580s, several Andalusian horses (p60) escaped and bred with the local ponies, adding beauty to this rugged breed.

Short ears · *Sturdy back* · *Refined head* · *Kindly eyes* · *Powerful legs and hindquarters*

HORSE PROFILE
Country: Ireland
Type: Pony **Height:** 12.2–14.2 hands
Colours: Grey, black, bay, brown, dun and occasionally roan, palomino or cream
Personality: Hardy, intelligent, dependable

These robust ponies have steady, sweet characters that make them suitable for riders of all ages. They are also used for showjumping, dressage and endurance riding.

EUROPE (North & West)

ICELANDIC

The first thing you need to know about the Icelandic is never call it a pony! Despite standing around 13 hands high, Icelanders always refer to this spirited and hardy breed as a horse.

The ancestors of these little horses first set hoof on the volcanic island of Iceland in the 9th century, when they were brought from Norway and Britain by Viking settlers. A law was soon passed forbidding the introduction of any other horse breeds to the country, meaning the Icelandic has stayed remarkably pure and unchanged to this day. Many Icelandics are left to roam freely and live semi-wild on the island.

Thick mane and tail
Strong legs
Stocky body
Has a short coat in summer and a thick, double coat in winter
Deep chest

Iceland's harsh climate and rocky landscape would be a challenge for the sturdiest of horses, but the Icelandic is perfectly adapted to thrive here. They are strong swimmers and sure-footed and grow a thick double coat in winter to protect them from the cold.

Traditionally, the horses were used by Icelandic people to herd sheep. Today, they take part in showjumping, cross-country racing and dressage. They are also used for tourist rides in Iceland – although small, they are happy carrying adult riders across the bumpiest of terrain.

HORSE PROFILE
Country: Iceland
Type: Pony **Height:** 12–14 hands
Colours: Any coat colour, including chestnut, dun, palomino, roan or black
Personality: Tough, free-spirited, intelligent

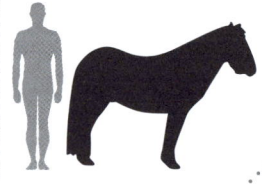

FJORD

The Fjord ('fee-ord') comes from Norway's west coast, where deep channels called fjords slice through mountains. These tough horses (despite being pony-sized, they are considered horses) have been shaped by this environment for 4,000 years. It's thought their ancestors were used by the Vikings as war horses before they became an essential part of Norwegian life, pulling ploughs on mountain farms and hauling logs through forests.

Kind expression
Small, alert ears

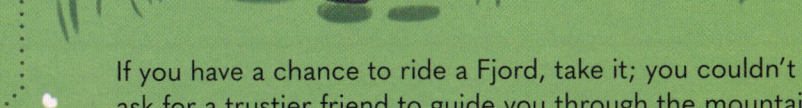

The horse's mane is usually cut short (or 'hogged') to show off the black stripe of hair that runs from the top of its head to the tip of its tail.

Round, barrel-like body
Arched neck
Wild horse markings, including a dorsal stripe and striped legs
Light feathering around hard hooves

HORSE PROFILE
Country: Norway
Type: Light **Height:** 13–14 hands
Colours: Dun
Personality: Courageous, robust, good-natured

If you have a chance to ride a Fjord, take it; you couldn't ask for a trustier friend to guide you through the mountains.

JUTLAND

This powerful breed comes from the Jutland Peninsula in Denmark. It's thought they were developed here from at least the 12th century, when knights relied on these heavy horses to carry them (and their armour) into battle.

By the mid-19th century, Jutlands had been refined to make them more suited to farm work. Breeders crossed local mares with a British stallion that was part Shire (p40) and part Suffolk Punch (p46). Today's Jutlands share the Suffolk's stout build, chestnut coat and soft nature.

Muscular and extremely powerful hindquarters
Short, arched neck
Round body
Wide, strong chest
Heavy feathering around feet
Short legs

HORSE PROFILE
Country: Denmark
Type: Heavy **Height:** 15–16.1 hands
Colours: Usually chestnut with flaxen mane and tail
Personality: Strong, hard-working, kind

WORKING HORSES

Imagine you lived 150 years ago. All around you would be busy horses hard at work – pulling coaches, barges and trains, ploughing the land and even delivering letters. Today, horses have been replaced by machines in most of their original roles, but many still perform important jobs around the world. Let's take a look at a few.

Many countries still rely on horses for farm work and transport. There are over 100 million working horses, ponies, donkeys and mules in the world today. They are not always well cared-for. Charities such as Brooke and World Horse Welfare work hard to help them.

ECO-FRIENDLY FARMING

In some parts of the world, horses are used as eco-friendly alternatives to tractors. The Suffolk Punch was developed on farms in England in the 18th century to pull enormous loads, but the breed declined when machines were introduced in the 20th century. Today, Suffolks are used to manage woods and farmland in parts of the UK. They help to keep the land healthy as they don't damage the soil as much as a vehicle's tyres. Plus, they provide a natural fertilizer through their poop!

POLICE HORSES

These sensible horses carry police officers on patrol, helping them see over crowds and quickly reach people who are hurt or causing trouble. Police officers around the world still use horses to keep the peace on streets or at busy events. Heavy horses, such as Percherons (p50), are valued for their powerful presence and calmness, while lighter breeds, such as Thoroughbreds (p41), are chosen for their speed.

Most horses were bred to do jobs. Heavy (or 'draught') horses did tough lifting and pulling tasks, lighter breeds were used to carry people or goods, and ponies worked in places where bigger horses couldn't go, such as mines.

THERAPY HORSES

These very special equines are trained to provide physical and emotional support to people. All sorts of breeds can be therapy horses, but they need to be gentle and steady. Horses with smooth gaits, such as Missouri Fox Trotters (p21), are used for riding therapies, helping people develop coordination and confidence. Due to their kind natures, heavy breeds, such as Clydesdales (p38), are often used for non-riding sessions, when people spend time stroking or walking a horse.

FILM AND TV HORSES

Horses regularly appear on our cinema and TV screens in everything from Western movies to period dramas. Months of careful training go into preparing horses for film roles. Some, like human extras, perform a role in the background and have to be calm and obedient so human actors can film their scenes without any hiccups. Others are specially trained to perform their own stunts, including rearing up, falling down and jumping over obstacles.

Horses have understudies and stunt doubles, just like human actors do. In the 2011 film War Horse the main horse character, Joey, was played by 14 different horses.

ROYAL HORSES

Horses add stateliness to royal ceremonies around the world. One of the most famous horsey spectacles is Trooping the Colour, which takes place in London, UK, every year to celebrate the British monarch's birthday. Over 200 horses march in this grand parade. These include Drum Horses, a heavy breed that carries a rider and a large set of drums – and is trained to stay steady while the drums are being played!

EUROPE (North & West)

SWEDISH WARMBLOOD

One of the world's oldest warmblood breeds, this handsome horse has its origins in the 17th century when Dutch, Spanish and English stallions, among others, were imported to Sweden and bred with local mares. The aim was to create top-notch horses for Swedish soldiers, which were swift and strong enough to cope with the battlefield.

These early horses shared similar characteristics but varied in size and appearance. In the 19th and 20th centuries, Thoroughbreds (p41), Arabs (p88), Hanoverians (p55) and Trakehners (p70) were brought in to make the breed more powerful. Nowadays, Swedish Warmbloods make outstanding riding and competition horses, which perform especially well in dressage and showjumping.

- Refined head with noble expression
- Sloping shoulders
- Medium-length back
- High-set tail
- Strong body
- Muscular legs

HORSE PROFILE
Country: Sweden
Type: Light **Height:** 16.2 hands
Colours: Any solid colour
Personality: Elegant, agile, fast

FINNISH HORSE

The Finnish Horse (or Finnhorse) is Finland's only horse breed. There were originally two types – the Draught, which was used to transport timber and plough fields, and the Universal, which had a lighter build and was bred for trotting races.

Modern Finn Horses are closer to the Universal in looks but they are still perfectly capable of lending a hoof on the farm when needed. This is a multitalented breed that is prized in Finnish riding schools for its calm nature, agility in the show ring and ability to pull a sleigh across a snowy plain with ease.

These compact horses are exceptionally strong and can pull up to twice their own weight!

- Compact, muscular body
- Flaxen tail and mane
- Short head with alert ears
- Sturdy legs
- Hard hooves with light feathering

Finnish Horses are used to take tourists on night-time sleigh rides to see the magical Northern Lights.

HORSE PROFILE
Country: Finland
Type: Light **Height:** 15.1 hands
Colours: Chestnut
Personality: Strong, hard-working, versatile

FRIESIAN

Are you looking for Black Beauty? Look no further! The jet-black Friesian is one of Europe's oldest and most iconic breeds. Its ancestors are thought to have been medieval war horses, which were created by crossing Dutch and Spanish breeds.

Friesians are powerfully built, agile and friendly, making them excellent all-rounders. Across the centuries, they have been used for farming and riding, and today, they perform well in dressage and harness racing. Because of their smart black coats and sensible nature, Friesians are often used to pull carriages at funerals and other important occasions.

Very long, glossy mane and tail – tail is low-set
Head and neck held proudly
Powerful shoulders
Sensible expression
Thick legs

Friesians are now bred to be all black. The only marking that is allowed is a white star on the horse's forehead.

HORSE PROFILE
- **Country:** Netherlands
- **Type:** Light **Height:** 15.3 hands
- **Colours:** Black
- **Personality:** Easy-going, calm, glamorous

BELGIAN WARMBLOOD

The Belgian Warmblood was created between the 1930s and 1950s by crossing Belgian farm horses with a Dutch breed called a Gelderlander. Selle Francais (p51), Thoroughbreds (p41) and Holsteiners (p54) were later added to create a powerful and agile sport horse.

Belgian Warmbloods have muscly legs and strong hindquarters, which makes them perfect for show jumping. A famous Belgian Warmblood called Big Ben won over 40 Grand Prix titles (the highest level of show jumping) during the 1980s and 1990s.

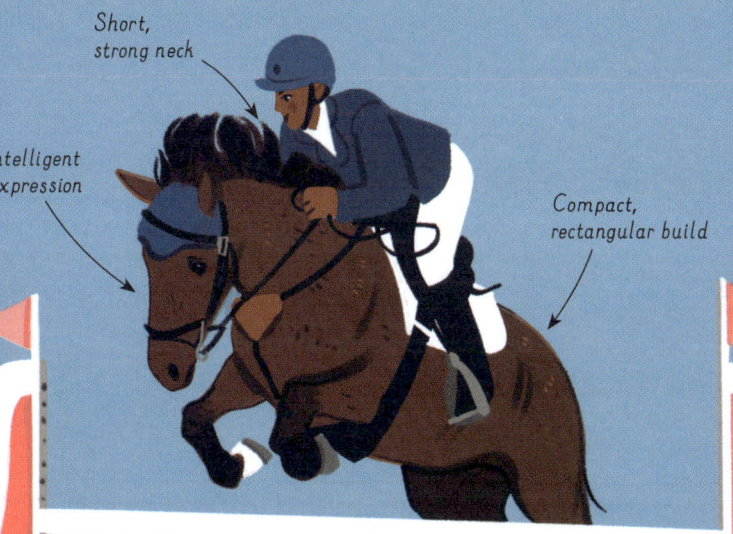

Short, strong neck
Intelligent expression
Compact, rectangular build
Long, strong legs

HORSE PROFILE
- **Country:** Belgium
- **Type:** Light **Height:** 16.2 hands
- **Colours:** Any solid colour, often bay, chestnut, grey, brown or black
- **Personality:** Fast, strong, spirited

EUROPE (North & West)

PERCHERON

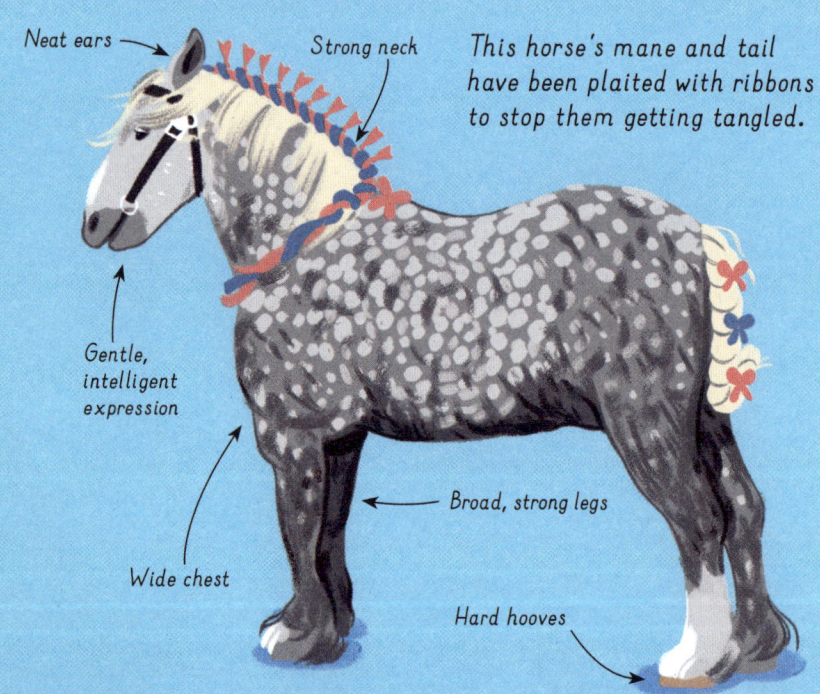

Neat ears · Strong neck · This horse's mane and tail have been plaited with ribbons to stop them getting tangled.
Gentle, intelligent expression
Broad, strong legs
Wide chest
Hard hooves

Strength, style and a sweet-nature: the Percheron has it all. Its ancestors are thought to have been large French horses that were crossed with Arabs (p88) and Spanish breeds in the Middle Ages (c.450–1450). This magical mix created one of the world's best-loved and most adaptable draught breeds.

Over the centuries, Percherons have carried knights into battle, farmed the land, pulled coaches and hauled machinery. They are traditionally dapple grey in colour – lighter horses were favoured by stagecoach drivers as they could be seen on the roads at night. Today, Percherons are used for farm work as well as appearing in shows and parades. If you visit Disneyland Paris, you might spot one of these dazzling horses pulling Cinderella's carriage!

HORSE PROFILE
Country: France **Type:** Heavy
Height: 16.2 hands
Colours: Traditionally dapple grey, though can also be black, bay, chestnut or roan
Personality: Obedient, adaptable, courageous

NORMAN COB

Thick mane and tail · Strong, large head · Short, powerful back
Muscular, stocky legs
Light feathering around feet

This compact horse comes from the lush pastures of Normandy in northern France. It's descended from a breed called a Carrossier Normand, created in the 17th century by crossing draught horses with lighter breeds, and was prized as a carriage horse.

By the 20th century, the breed had been split into two types – lighter horses for riding and heavier horses (the Norman Cobs) for farm work. Norman Cobs can still be seen on farms in northern France. They also make excellent horses for vaulting (gymnastics on horseback) due to their broad, strong backs.

HORSE PROFILE
Country: France
Type: Heavy **Height:** 15.3–16.2 hands
Colours: Typically chestnut, bay or seal brown (brown body with darker legs, mane and tail)
Personality: Sensible, strong, versatile

Carrossier Normands were used by French postmen in the 19th century; they had the stamina to pull a cart for hours and the patience to wait quietly while letters were delivered.

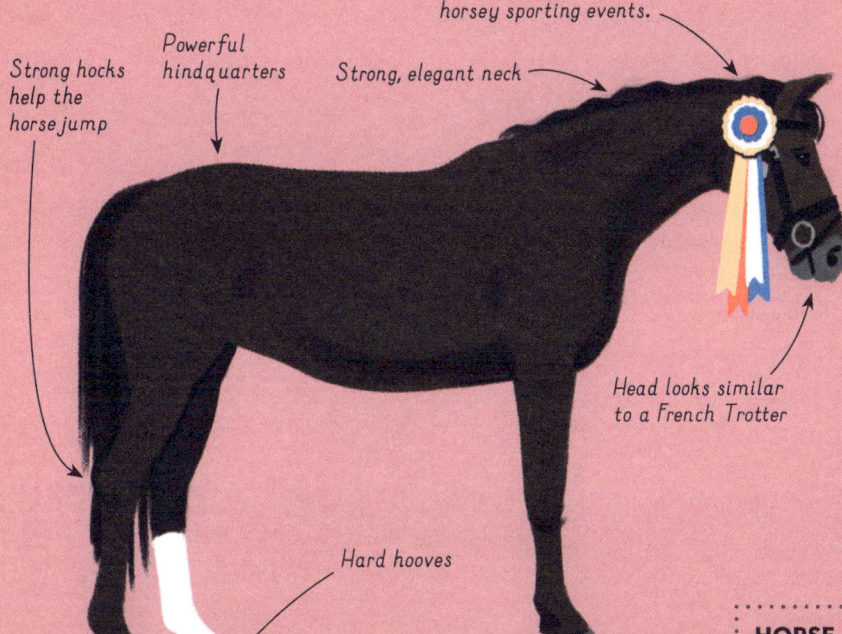

Strong hocks help the horse jump

Powerful hindquarters

Strong, elegant neck

This horse is wearing a rosette – a decoration made of ribbons awarded as a prize in horsey sporting events.

Head looks similar to a French Trotter

Hard hooves

SELLE FRANCAIS

During the 19th century, stables throughout France began importing Thoroughbreds (p41) to breed with their local mares and create elegant riding horses. By the early 20th century, several distinct types had emerged, notably from Normandy and western and eastern France. These crossbreeds were grouped together under one name in 1958 – the Selle Francais (or French Saddlehorse).

French Trotters (below) have been used to refine the Selle Francais over the last 70 years and create a nimble horse that excels in showjumping. These sporty horses frequently rank among the world's best jumpers, scooping up medals at Olympic Games and other international championships.

HORSE PROFILE
Country: France **Type:** Light
Height: Usually over 16 hands
Colours: Bay or chestnut
Personality: Athletic, strong, graceful

FRENCH TROTTER

The French Trotter was developed in the early 19th century for a type of horse racing called trotting. During trotting, a horse must perform an unbroken trot, moving its legs in diagonal pairs. The horse either pulls a lightweight cart (called a sulky) while trotting or is ridden by a jockey.

Breeders in Normandy used a wide range of horses to perfect the French Trotter. They crossed local mares with Thoroughbreds (p41) for stamina and Norfolk Trotters for their trotting skills. American Standardbreds (p17) were later added for extra speed.

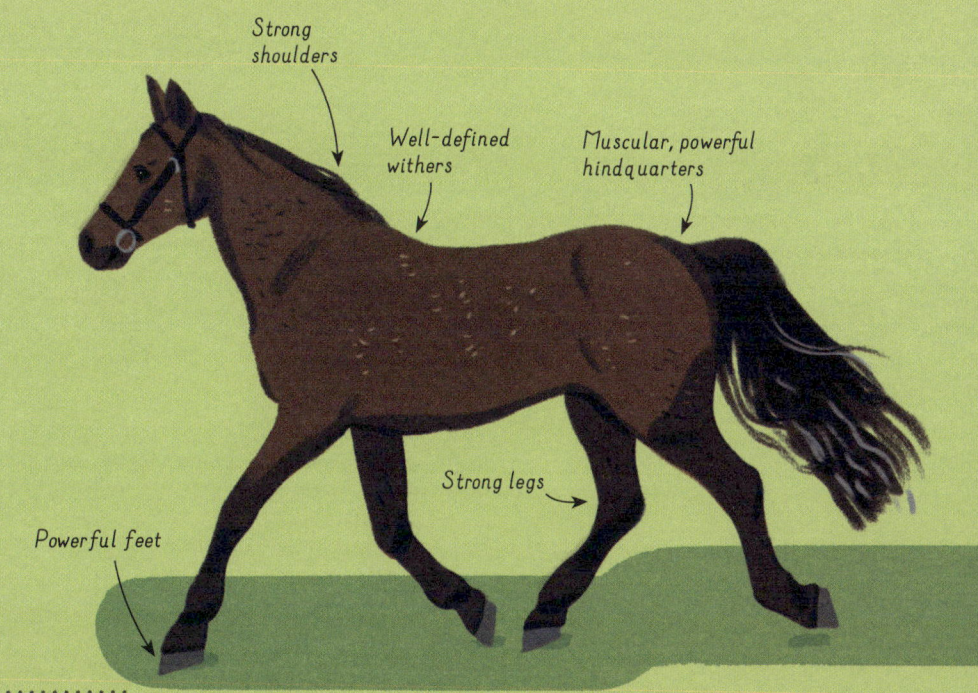

Strong shoulders

Well-defined withers

Muscular, powerful hindquarters

Powerful feet

Strong legs

HORSE PROFILE
Country: France
Type: Light **Height:** 16.2 hands
Colours: Chestnut, brown or bay
Personality: Tough, athletic, focused

EUROPE (North & West)

ARDENNAIS

The Ardennais is one of the biggest horses on the stable block. This chunky breed is more thick-set than any other draught horse, with short, tree-trunk-like legs to maximise its pulling power.

These burly horses come from the Ardennes region, which covers parts of northern France, Belgium, Germany and Luxembourg. Since ancient times, the horses of this rugged landscape have been admired for their strength and hardiness – the Roman leader Julius Caesar was a fan.

Until the mid-20th century, the Ardennais was mainly a war horse. These brave horses carried knights in the medieval Crusades (1095–1291), lugged guns to Russia for the French Emperor Napoleon in the 19th century and hauled supplies in both World Wars. Nowadays, they are used in France for farm and forestry work, such as hauling logs (as shown here).

Despite their tank-like looks, Ardennais are gentle souls and will happily be handled by children. They make wonderful therapy horses due to their calm presence.

Muscular body

Broad, short back

Short, thick legs

Thick feathering around feet

Fairly small feet compared to large body size

HORSE PROFILE
Country: France
Type: Heavy **Height:** Over 17 hands
Colours: Black, brown, bay or grey
Personality: Loyal, hard-working, kindly

BRETON

This sleek and sturdy horse has its roots in Brittany, a region in north-west France. There are two official versions of the Breton – a lighter type called the Breton Postier and a heavier type called the Breton Heavy Draught (pictured).

Both Bretons are hard-working horses with enormous stamina. The Postier was originally developed for light farm work and as a military horse, while the Heavy Draught did the tougher lifting and pulling tasks. The Heavy Draught is the more common of the two and is often used on vineyards in the south of France to plough fields and transport boxes of grapes.

Bretons were used by farmers to harvest seaweed along the Brittany coast.

- Sloping shoulders
- Compact body
- Thick, arched neck
- Glossy coat
- Short, thick legs
- Light feathering around feet

HORSE PROFILE
Country: France **Type:** Heavy
Height: 15.1–16 hands
Colours: Usually chestnut with a flaxen mane and tail
Personality: Willing, hardy, friendly

BOULONNAIS

The rare and beautiful Boulonnais comes from the north coast of France. Its ancestors were developed at the time of the medieval Crusades (1095–1291) by crossing local working breeds with lighter German breeds to create strong, nimble war horses.

In the 17th century, Spanish horses and Arabs (p88) were added, giving the breed an extra dash of elegance. There are two types of Boulonnais – a lighter type, originally used to transport carts of fish swiftly from seaside towns to Paris, and a heavier type, which did the farm work.

- Small, refined head reflects Arab and Thoroughbred ancestry
- Broad back
- Glossy mane and tail
- Deep, powerful chest
- Marble-like pattern on coat
- Muscly legs

The Boulonnais is unusually pretty and dainty for a heavy breed.

HORSE PROFILE
Country: France
Type: Heavy **Height:** 15.1–17.3 hands
Colours: Usually grey but can be chestnut or black too
Personality: Elegant, powerful, energetic

EUROPE (North & West)

OLDENBURGER

The elegant Oldenburger is named after an ancient region of north-west Germany. It was developed by local aristocrats in the 17th century by crossing Friesians (p49) with Spanish and Italian horses. These early Oldenburgers were robust but graceful and were used to pull carriages as well as work on farms.

In the 20th century, Thoroughbreds (p41) were added to transform the breed into a sleek sport horse. Although they are not as fast as German breeds such as the Hanoverian (see opposite), Oldenburgers make stunning show jumping and dressage horses thanks to their powerful builds and eager-to-please natures.

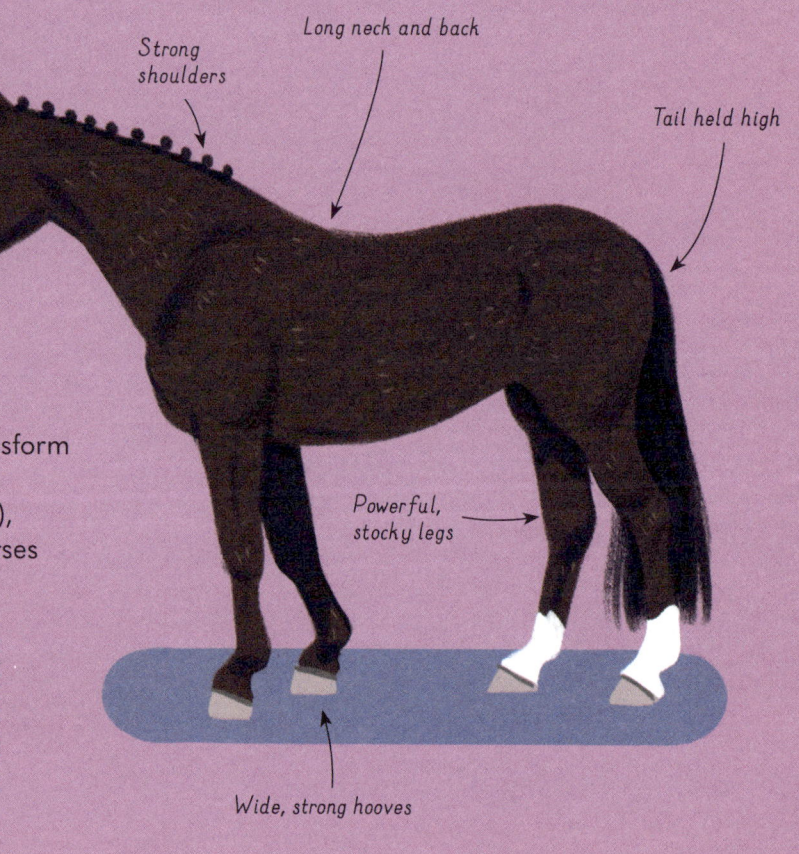

Strong shoulders
Long neck and back
Tail held high
Powerful, stocky legs
Wide, strong hooves

HORSE PROFILE
Country: Germany
Type: Light **Height:** 16.2–17.2 hands
Colours: Usually black, brown or bay
Personality: Strong, obedient, stylish

Small head with refined features
Well-defined withers
Strong back
Powerful hindquarters
Arched neck

HOLSTEINER

The Holsteiner has had many roles during its 700-year history. Its ancestors were small horses that lived in north Germany, where they were used by monks to ride through misty marshes. These horses were later mixed with Arabs (p88) and Spanish breeds to produce agile farm workers. By the 19th century, Holsteiners had been crossed with English coach horses and put to work pulling carriages.

In the 1940s, the Holsteiner was reinvented for the final time. Thoroughbreds (p41) were added to create horses that were tall, precise and perfect for showjumping. Ever since, these springy athletes have ruled the world's showjumping scene.

HORSE PROFILE
Country: Germany
Type: Light **Height:** 16–17 hands
Colours: Any solid colour, but black, bay, brown or grey are common
Personality: Bold, good-natured, graceful

HANOVERIAN

This noble-looking horse was developed in the 1730s by George II, the king of Great Britain, who set up a famous stable near his home city of Hanover in Germany. There, local horses were crossed with German, English, Italian and Spanish breeds to create the Hanoverian.

Hanoverians were originally used to pull coaches, carry soldiers and, sometimes, double-up as farm horses. In the 1940s, Trakehners (p70) and Thoroughbreds (p41) were introduced to turn the breed into a sport horse. Today, these stately horses excel at dressage, showjumping and eventing.

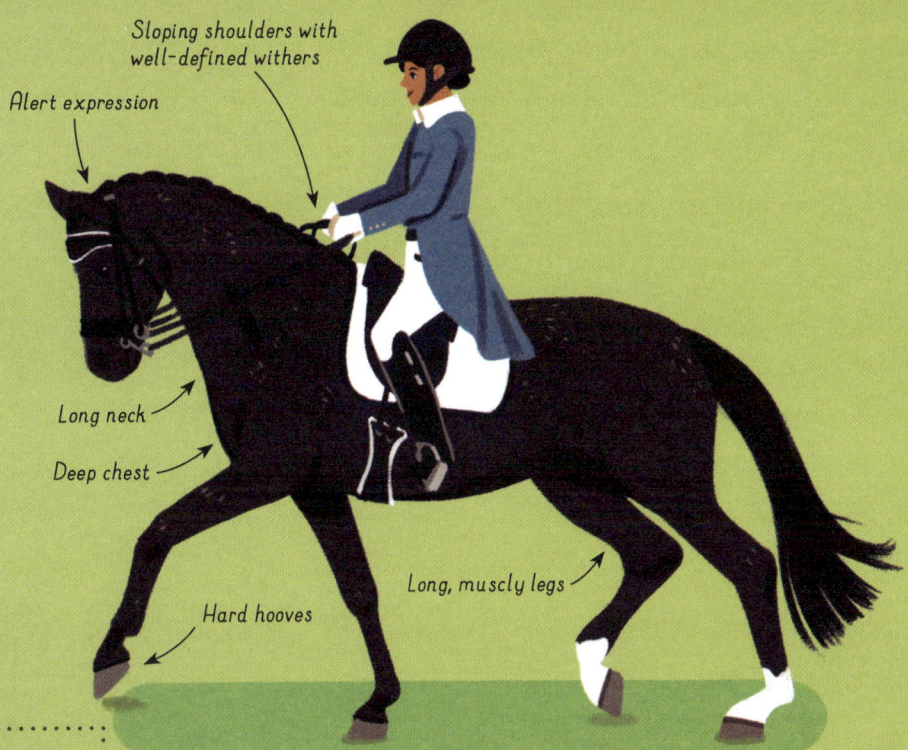

Sloping shoulders with well-defined withers
Alert expression
Long neck
Deep chest
Hard hooves
Long, muscly legs

HORSE PROFILE
Country: Germany
Type: Light **Height:** 15.3–17.1 hands
Colours: Any solid colour, but black, bay, chestnut or grey are common
Personality: Calm, athletic, elegant

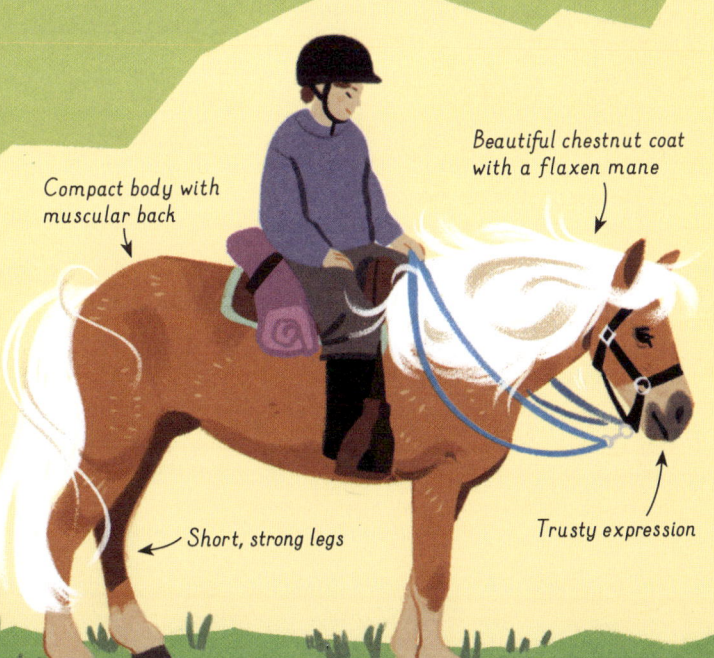

Compact body with muscular back
Beautiful chestnut coat with a flaxen mane
Short, strong legs
Trusty expression
Small, hard hooves

HAFLINGER

Are you planning a trek up a mountain? Then take a Haflinger with you! These small horses come from the Tyrolean Mountains between Austria and Italy. There, they work on farms, lug logs through forests and help travellers navigate treacherous paths. Strong and remarkably sure-footed, the Haflinger is the ultimate mountaineering buddy.

The breed was officially established in the 1870s, when a local mare bred with an Arab (p88) stallion. Their stunning golden foal (called Folie) became the founding father of the modern Haflinger breed. Nowadays, Haflingers are popular around the world for trail riding and dressage, and make top therapy horses because of their steady and extremely kind characters.

HORSE PROFILE
Country: Austria
Type: Light **Height:** 13.2–15 hands
Colours: Chestnut
Personality: Reliable, gentle, intelligent

FREE-ROAMING HORSES

While most domestic horses live and work alongside people, some trot a wilder path. Domestic horses that live in the wild with little human contact are known as feral horses. Domestic horses that are left to roam freely in the wild but have an owner are called semi-feral horses. Herds of feral and semi-feral horses are found in many parts of the world, and they have often adapted to survive in unique environments. Here are just a few of the planet's free-roaming breeds.

MUSTANG (USA)

Nothing conjures up the spirit of the American West like the sight of a herd of Mustangs galloping across a wide, open plain. These feral horses have dashed across the deserts and prairies of the USA since the 17th century, when Spanish and other European settlers turned their spare horses loose.

Today, there are around 86,000 Mustangs in America. Because they have bred freely with one another, they come in a range of colours and sizes (although most are between 14–15 hands high). They are fast, hardy and healthy horses and can be tamed for leisure riding and ranch work.

CHINCOTEAGUE (USA)

Despite being named after Chincoteague Island on America's East Coast, these ponies live on neighbouring Assateague Island. Legend tells how a Spanish ship was wrecked there in the 17th century and a herd of plucky ponies swam to shore. In reality, their ancestors were probably abandoned there by settlers.

Chincoteague ponies eat tough beach grass and seaweeds, which are high in salt. Because of this, they drink twice as much water as other horses, meaning their tummies look bloated. This doesn't affect their health or agility; each year, they are rounded up and swim to Chincoteague so they can be checked over by a vet.

CAMARGUE (FRANCE)

A wetland in the south of France is the stomping ground of a very special group of horses. Camargues are descended from prehistoric equines and are thought to have been influenced by Spanish, Arabian and African breeds over the last 3,000 years. These robust horses have large hooves that are flatter and more water-resistant than other breeds and an ability to survive on chewy marshland plants. Camargues love being in water and can often be seen splashing through the lagoons. Although many Camargues live a wild existence, some have been tamed by local farmers, called *gardians*, who use them to round up their black cattle that graze on the marshes.

EXMOOR AND DARTMOOR PONIES (UK)

It is believed that the Exmoor pony has its roots in ancient ponies that were domesticated by the Celts (c.400 BCE). The first record of ponies on Exmoor, a remote moor in Devon, England, dates from 1086.

Many are now kept as pets, but some still live semi-feral on the moor. These tough ponies are perfectly adapted to life in a cold climate. They grow a woolly, double-coat in winter, have a fan of thick hairs at the top of their tail (called a 'snow chute') to deflect water, and fleshy rims around their eyes (called 'toad' eye) to keep the rain out.

Dartmoor Pony

Exmoor Pony

The Dartmoor is another beautiful semi-feral pony that can still be found roaming the valleys and hills of its windswept Devon home. Like the Exmoor, its ancestors were ponies domesticated by ancient Britons. However, over the years, Dartmoors have been used widely as riding ponies and mining ponies and crossed with other breeds (such as Welsh Ponies).

Feral and semi-feral horses live freely in herds, usually made up of a stallion, mares and their foals. These horses find their own food and shelter rather than rely on people to look after them. Other feral and semi-feral horses include the Icelandic (p44), Brumby (p106) and Skyrian (p65).

EUROPE (South & East)

Welcome to a land where horsey worlds collide. Many horses and ponies in southern and eastern Europe share histories with their cousins in the north of the continent, but they also reflect the influence of Asian and African breeds. As a result, this part of Europe is home to some of the world's most exciting and extravagant horses. In this chapter, we'll meet spectacular showjumpers like Italy's Salerno, graceful carriage horses like Czechia's Kladruber, and perhaps the most breathtaking breed of all – Slovenia's dancing Lipizzaner.

Sorraia horses are currently being used in rewilding projects in Portugal. Through their grazing, the horses help to maintain natural habitats and help other wildlife thrive.

SORRAIA
PORTUGAL

ITALIAN HEAVY DRAUGHT
ITALY

LUSITANO
PORTUGAL

ANDALUSIAN
SPAIN

Thanks to their glamorous looks and intelligence, Andalusians are often used for film work. Two Andalusian stallions called Domero and Blanco starred as the magical Shadowfax in the Lord of the Rings films.

EUROPE (South & East)

Each spring, the city of Jerez in Andalusia hosts a festival that celebrates horses. People in traditional Spanish dress parade through the city streets with their Andalusians, as shown here.

- Muscular neck
- Large, strong chest
- Elegant but compact build
- Strong legs
- Long, thick mane and tail

ANDALUSIAN

Twenty thousand years ago in what is now Spain, a prehistoric person picked up a brush and carefully painted a horse on to the wall of a cave. That horse was a distant ancestor of today's Andalusian.

The breed was developed properly from the 15th century when Spanish royals set up stables in Andalusia, in southern Spain. Many of these stables were run by monks, who left written records of the breed's development. Local horses were bred with Barbs (p76) from North Africa to create beautiful equines for Spanish kings, queens and armies to ride.

Andalusians were given as gifts to other European aristocrats, helping the breed to become popular outside of Spain. Their strong presence and proud way of walking makes them ideal for classical dressage (called *haute école*), as well as stunning riding horses.

HORSE PROFILE
Country: Spain
Type: Light **Height:** 15–15.2 hands
Colours: Usually grey or bay, but can come in other colours, such as black, palomino or chestnut
Personality: Intelligent, strong, beautiful

LUSITANO

The Lusitano is a close cousin of the Andalusian (see opposite) and shares its ancient roots. In fact, the horses were considered one breed until the 1960s.

Historically, Lusitanos were used as war horses and for general riding, driving and classical dressage – where horses perform a series of elaborate jumps, hops and dances. Specialist schools, such as the Portuguese School of Equestrian Art in Lisbon, the country's capital city, still put on classical dressage performances using Lusitanos.

Curved head
Muscular shoulders and strong chest
Thick mane and tail
Arched neck
Elegant, compact build

HORSE PROFILE
Country: Portugal
Type: Light **Height:** 15–16 hands
Colours: Usually grey or bay
Personality: Affectionate, hard-working, graceful

SORRAIA

The sturdy Sorraia is one of the world's rarest and most endangered breeds. These little horses are named after the Sorraia River in Portugal, where a zoologist found a herd in the 1920s.

The Sorraia are thought to have lived wild on the plains and marshes along the river for thousands of years, although local people would occasionally tame them and use them for herding cattle and farm work. Today, there are only around 200 Sorraia left and they live in protected herds.

Alert ears
Curved head
Slender neck
Long legs
Primitive markings typical of wild horses, such as a dorsal stripe along the back and striped markings on legs

HORSE PROFILE
Country: Portugal
Type: Light **Height:** 14.1–14.3 hands
Colours: Usually dun
Personality: Independent, tough, agile

EUROPE (South & East)

ITALIAN HEAVY DRAUGHT

The Italian Heavy Draught comes from the wide plains of northern Italy. It was developed in the second half of the 19th century by farmers who needed strong but quick-moving horses to help them in the fields. They crossed local mares with various European heavy breeds – notably Bretons (p53) – to create their perfect horse.

Italian Heavy Draughts are prized for their speediness, even when pulling heavy loads. In Italy, they are also called the Tiro Pesante Rapido, which means 'fast farm horse'.

Refined head, *Big, bright eyes*, *Muscular neck*, *Deep chest*, *Short, strong legs*, *Large feet*

HORSE PROFILE
Country: Italy
Type: Heavy **Height:** 15–16 hands
Colours: Usually chestnut
Personality: Gentle, strong, fast

MAREMMANO

This rustic breed comes from the Maremma region on the west coast of Italy. Renowned for their cattle skills, these horses have helped Italian cowboys (called *butteri*) round up livestock in the area's hills and marshlands for centuries. Today, *butteri* still use Maremmanos to round up long-horned cattle in the Maremma National Park.

Many breeds are thought to have been used to develop the Maremmano, including Spanish, Neapolitan, Thoroughbred (p41), Arab (p88) and Barb (p76). Maremmanos are not very quick, but they make great riding buddies and police horses due to their strength and willing natures.

Short back, *Strong hindquarters*, *Low-set tail*, *Long, sturdy legs*, *Intelligent expression*

HORSE PROFILE
Country: Italy
Type: Light **Height:** 15.3 hands
Colours: Any solid colour, but usually bay, brown, black or chestnut
Personality: Hard-working, calm, tough

SALERNO

This athletic horse comes from the southwest of Italy and evolved from a now-extinct breed called a Neapolitan. The Neapolitan developed around the city of Naples between the 16th and 19th centuries and was one of the finest riding horses of its time. These horses were mixed with Spanish, Arab (p88), Barb (p76) and, later, Thoroughbreds (p41) to create the sleek and speedy Salerno.

Salernos are rare today, but they used to be popular showjumping horses. A famous Italian rider called Raimondo d'Inzeo won a gold medal at the 1960 Olympic Games riding a Salerno called Posillipo.

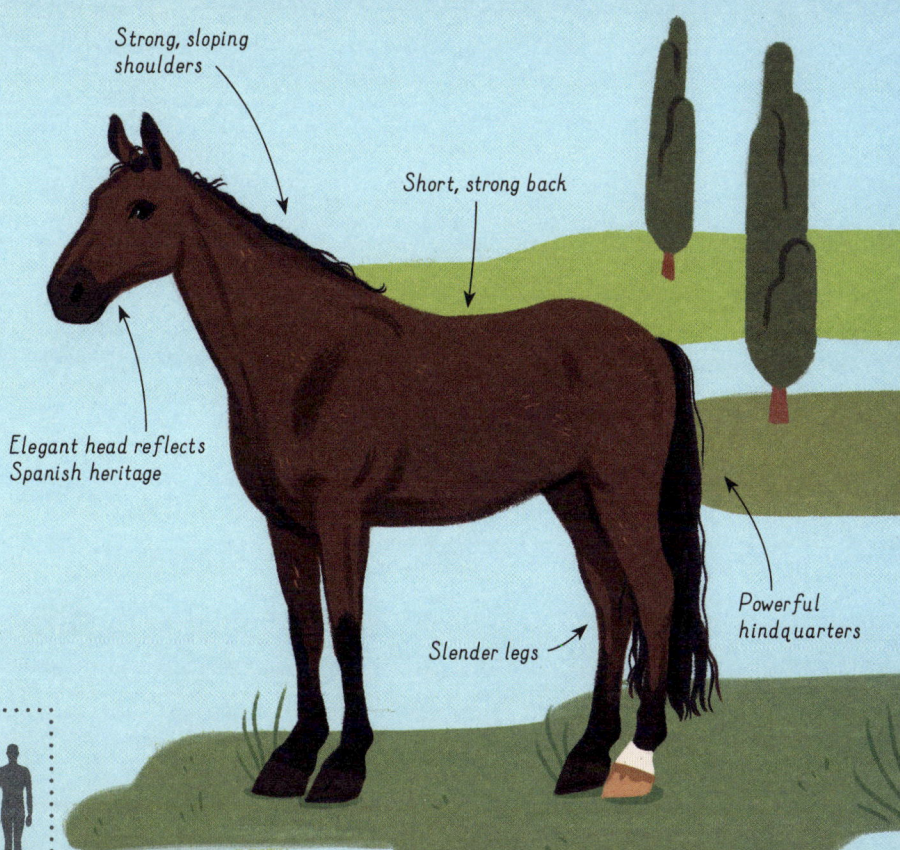

HORSE PROFILE
Country: Italy
Type: Light **Height:** 16 hands
Colours: Usually black, bay or chestnut
Personality: Sensible, gentle, agile

MURGESE

The impressive Murgese comes from the wooded hills and dry plateaus of Puglia in southeast Italy. Its ancestors were ridden by Italian soldiers in the 15th and 16th centuries, but then the breed declined. Fans of the Murgese started a breeding programme in the 1920s to save the breed and find it a new job as a light draught horse on farms.

Murgese are still used for farm work in Puglia, as well as for trekking and cross-country riding. They are also often crossed with donkeys to produce strong mules.

HORSE PROFILE
Country: Italy
Type: Light **Height:** 15–16 hands
Colours: Usually black or blue roan
Personality: Hardy, active, even-tempered

EUROPE (South & East)

LIPIZZANER

No horse combines style and skill quite like the Lipizzaner. These dreamy horses are famous for their spectacular dance shows at the Spanish Riding School in Vienna, Austria. For over 450 years, the school has specialised in a type of classical dressage called *haute école* (high school). During performances, a fleet of sparkling-white Lipizzaners display breathtaking leaps, jumps and moves to music.

Although the horses are associated with Vienna, the Lipizzaner originated in the mountain village of Lipica in Slovenia. The breed was developed there in the 16th and 17th centuries, when classical riding schools became fashionable across Europe. Breeders used a mix of Spanish horses, Barbs (p76), Arabs (p88) and Neapolitans to create these magical, nimble-hoofed horses.

Elegant head
Low withers
Silky mane and tail
Muscular, compact body
Strong, hard feet

This Lipizzaner is putting on an acrobatic show. When not performing, the horses are cared for in the Spanish Riding School's stables. In the summer, they take breaks from training at special riding centres in the Austrian countryside.

HORSE PROFILE
Country: Slovenia **Type:** Light
Height: 14.2–15.2 hands
Colours: Grey-white
Personality: Elegant, athletic, intelligent

Traditionally, only Lipizzaner stallions perform at the Spanish School. It takes about six years for a Lipizzaner to complete its training, which is gentle and guided by what the horse feels comfortable with. A small number of talented stallions are taught the most difficult moves, in which all four of the horse's feet leave the floor (called 'airs above the ground').

PINDOS

These tough ponies come from the rugged Pindus Mountains in northern Greece. For centuries, they have been used by local farmers for ploughing, lugging timber and pack work, as well as for general riding. They are also bred with donkeys to create strong mules.

Their origins are uncertain but it's thought they may have some Asian heritage. Pindos are perfectly adapted to their mountain home, with hard, nimble hooves for clambering over rocks, incredible endurance and an ability to survive on minimal food when times are tough.

HORSE PROFILE
Country: Greece
Type: Pony **Height:** 12 hands
Colours: Typically bay, black or grey
Personality: Strong, stubborn, hardy

SKYRIAN

Meet the small but mighty Skyrian. It's thought these little horses were once found across ancient Greece (1200 BCE–323 BCE). Legend tells how they pulled the chariot of the hero Achilles, and equines that look like Skyrians are carved into the marble that decorate a famous ancient temple, the Parthenon, in Athens.

Today, only around 200 of these very rare horses remain on the Greek island of Skyros. To help protect them, conservation teams have started a breeding programme and are training them for activities such as riding and therapy projects.

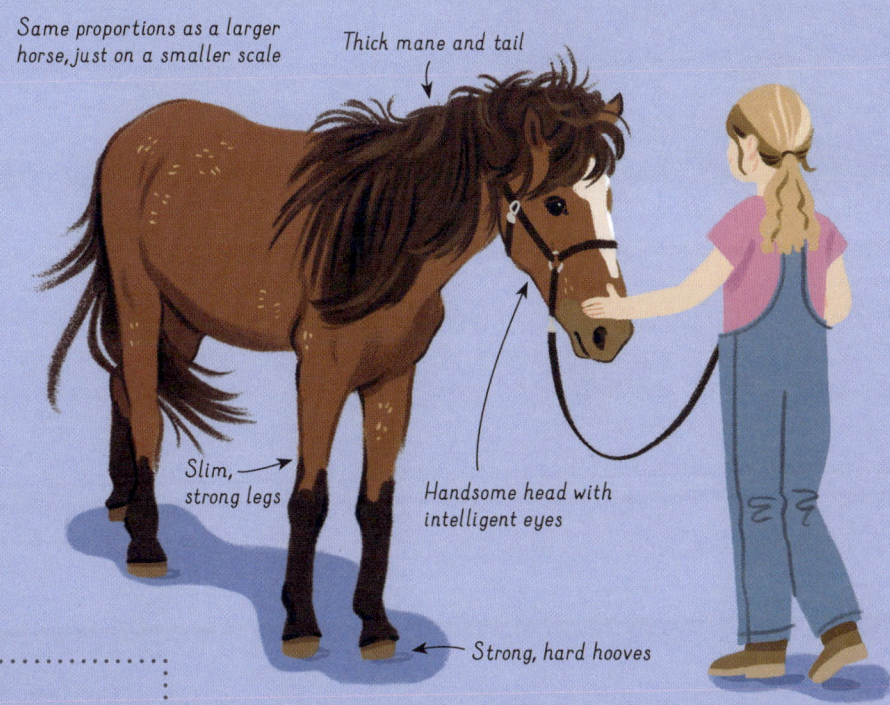

It's thought that the Skyrians' ancestors were normal-sized – they became smaller over hundreds of years to adapt to the island's rugged environment.

HORSE PROFILE
Country: Greece
Type: Pony **Height:** 10 hands
Colours: Any solid colour, usually bay, dun, black or dark brown
Personality: Friendly, tough, clever

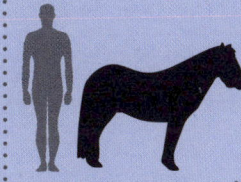

EUROPE (South & East)

SHAGYA-ARABIAN

In the 9th century, an ancient tribe of skilled horse-people began living in the plains and mountains of Hungary in Central Europe. Ever since, Hungary has cherished its deep connection with horses. In the 18th and 19th centuries, the country's breeds were admired across Europe, and the Shagya-Arabian was considered a particular treasure.

The breed is named after Shagya, an Arab stallion bought by the Hungarian king in the 1830s and raised by the Bani Sakher people in the Syrian Desert. All of today's Shagya-Arabians can trace their roots back to him.

- Large, expressive eyes
- Dipped (or 'dished') face
- Broad, muscly chest
- Similar build to an Arab horse but taller
- High-set tail

This classy horse was developed at Babolna, a royal stud farm, in the 1780s by crossing Arab (p88) stallions with heavier, Hungarian mares. The aim was to create a practical version of the Arab that could carry soldiers into battle and pull carriages with ease and elegance.

The features that made the breed such a good cavalry and carriage horse 200 years ago make it a superb sport horse today. Combining stamina, presence and speed, Shagya-Arabians are particularly well suited to dressage, endurance riding and jumping.

HORSE PROFILE
Country: Hungary
Type: Light **Height:** 15–16 hands
Colours: Usually grey, but can also be bay, chestnut, black or roan
Personality: Elegant, tough, fast

NONIUS

The noble Nonius was developed in a famous royal stud farm in Mezőhegyes, Hungary, in the 1780s. A stallion called Nonius was brought from Normandy and bred with Arab (p88), Thoroughbred (p41), Lipizzaner (p64) and Spanish horses to establish the breed.

Developed as military mounts, Nonius horses were used for farm work into the 20th century. They can still sometimes be seen pulling ploughs on Hungary's great plains, as shown in the top right image. They also make good horses for leisure riding. But these horses are rare, with only around 500 alive today.

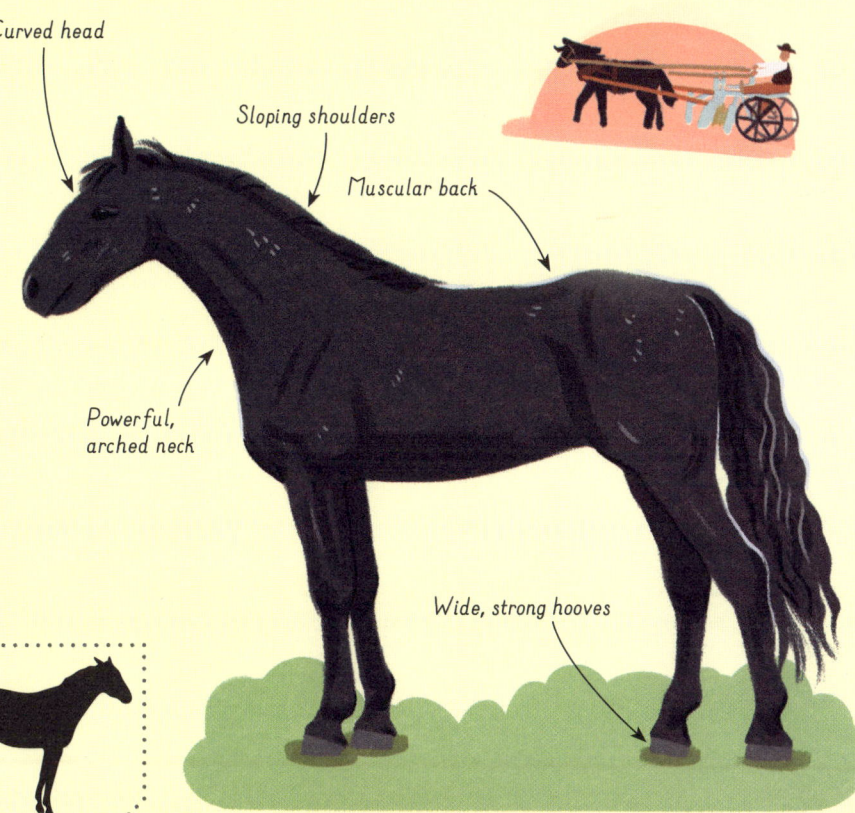

HORSE PROFILE
Country: Hungary
Type: Light **Height:** 15.1–16.1 hands
Colours: Black, brown or dark bay
Personality: Strong, hard-working, gentle

HUCUL

The name Hucul comes from a Romanian word meaning 'rebel' or 'outlaw', and it reflects this pony's tough personality. An ancient breed, Huculs are descended from a prehistoric horse called a Tarpan and have been galloping around the Carpathian Mountains in Central Europe for hundreds of years.

In that time, Huculs have been used to pull carts, transport goods over the mountains, haul timber in forests, work on hilltop farms and carry soldiers.

HORSE PROFILE
Country: Hungary, Slovakia, Czechia, Ukraine, Poland and Romania
Type: Pony **Height:** 13–14 hands
Colours: Usually bay, dun, black or chestnut
Personality: Hardy, calm, sure-footed

MYTHICAL HORSES

Horses have galloped into our imaginations and trotted into our folk tales for thousands of years. In some myths, horses are symbols of beauty or bravery; in others, they possess otherworldly powers. Each story reflects our fascination and deep bond with these amazing animals.

MAGICAL UNICORNS

The unicorn is the most famous magical horsey creature of all. In Europe, unicorn myths can be traced back to an ancient Greek historian called Ctesias (c.400 BCE), who wrote about an animal with a pearl-white body and a horn with healing powers.

Ctesias was probably describing a rhinoceros, but the image endured and spread throughout Western culture. In medieval Europe (c.400–1400 CE), many people believed that unicorns were real. Artworks of the time depict huntsmen battling through dark forests to find these enchanting equines.

THE MYSTERIOUS QILIN

A similar myth appeared in ancient China around 2700 BCE. The Chinese version of the unicorn is called the *qilin* ('chee-lin'). It has a horse-like body, a dragon head, a coat covered in scales and a single horn. Like the European unicorn, the qilin is a gentle, wise and shy creature.

In medieval Europe, people would pay a lot of money for special cups that were said to be made from unicorn horn, which was thought to protect the drinker from poisons. These cups were actually made from the tusks of real-life animals such as rhinos or narwhals.

FLYING FREE

Hot on the hooves of the unicorn is another iconic magical horse – Pegasus. In ancient Greek mythology, Pegasus is born from the blood of Medusa, a monster with snakes for hair. Pegasus is later tamed by a Greek hero, named Bellerophon, and the pair go on many adventures together.

Pegasus is one of many winged horses found in myths around the world. The Turkic cultures of Western and Central Asia, for example, celebrate a flying horse called Tulpar, who represents speed, strength and freedom. In East Asia, the *qianlima* is a magical horse that can travel 1,000 Chinese miles (500 km) in a single day thanks to its powerful wings.

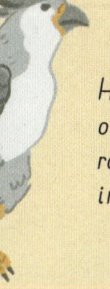

Hippogriffs have the front half of an eagle and the back half of a horse. A hippogriff called Buckbeak plays an important role in the Harry Potter books, but the creature was actually invented by an Italian poet in the 16th century!

CUNNING KELPIES

Some horse stories have a darker side. The kelpie is a shape-shifting water spirit from Scottish folklore. Kelpies are said to live in lakes and rivers where they take the form of beautiful horses that lure travellers to their doom.

As soon as a human sits on a kelpie, they are trapped by the horse's sticky coat and carried off into the water to be eaten! The good news is that kelpies have a weak spot – their bridle. If you can keep hold of a kelpie's bridle, you can control the horse and escape.

EUROPE (South & East)

UKRAINIAN SADDLE HORSE

This strong horse was developed after World War II in the region of Dnipro in central Ukraine. Breeders crossed Hungarian mares with Trakehners (see below), Hanoverians (p55) and Thoroughbreds (p41). A few stud farms also used a now-extinct breed called a Russian Saddle Horse – any Ukrainian Saddle Horse with this heritage is considered particularly special.

Ukrainian Saddle Horses have appeared at Olympic Games and World and European Championships. As well as being nimble dressage and showjumping horses, they make friendly riding horses.

HORSE PROFILE
Country: Ukraine **Type:** Light
Height: 15.7–16.2 hands
Colours: Usually bay, brown or chestnut
Personality: Calm, well-behaved, powerful

Expressive eyes
Well-defined withers
Long back
Solid legs
Muscular body with broad chest

TRAKEHNER

This breed is named after the town of Trakehen in modern-day Russia. It was developed in the 18th century, when the town was part of East Prussia (now split between Russia, Lithuania and Poland).

Local Lithuanian horses, which were renowned for their hardiness and intelligence, were crossed with sporty breeds, such as Thoroughbreds (p41) and Arabs (p88). Originally used to pull coaches and carry soldiers, today the Trakehner is a fantastic jumper and dressage horse. Its springy way of walking makes it look especially elegant in the show ring.

High-set tail
Sloping shoulders
Expressive eyes
Long neck
Powerful hindquarters

HORSE PROFILE
Country: Lithuania and Russia
Type: Light **Height:** 15.2–17 hands
Colours: Any solid colour, usually chestnut, bay, black or grey
Personality: Spirited, strong, graceful

WIELKOPOLSKI

Named after a region in west-central Poland, the Wielkopolski (you say it 've-el-ko-pol-ski') is a fairly modern breed. It was developed in 1964 by crossing two now-extinct Polish breeds – the Poznan, a heavier farm horse, and the Mazury, a lighter riding horse closely related to the Trakehner (see opposite).

There are two distinct types of Wielkopolski. The most popular version is a light, athletic horse used for dressage and showjumping. The other is a heavier type, bred for driving and general riding.

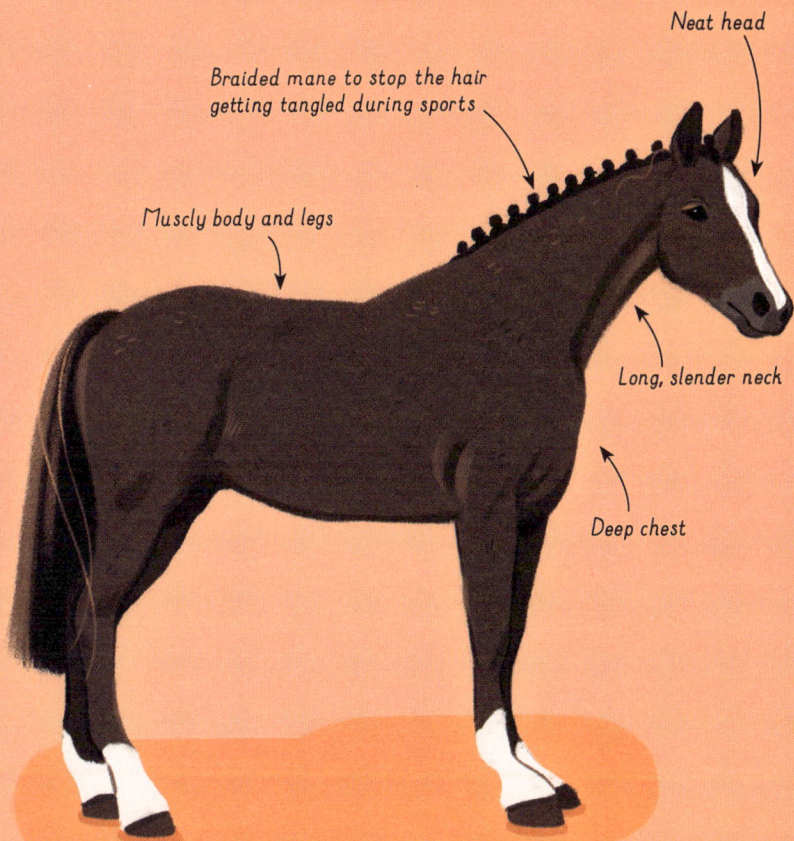

Neat head
Braided mane to stop the hair getting tangled during sports
Muscly body and legs
Long, slender neck
Deep chest

HORSE PROFILE
Country: Poland
Type: Light **Height:** 15.2–16.2 hands
Colours: Grey, bay, chestnut or black
Personality: Hardy, calm, elegant

KLADRUBER

The Kladruber was created for a very special purpose – to pull carriages for kings and queens. This rare breed can be traced to the 16th century, when a stud farm was set up in the town of Kladruby in Czechia for the Habsburg monarchy (the royal family who ruled much of Europe at the time).

Kladrubers come in only two colours – grey horses were traditionally used to pull royal carriages while black horses were used for important religious people and at funerals. Today, these stately equines are used as police and riding horses in Czechia.

Curved head (called a Roman nose)
Arched, elegant neck
Upright shoulders
Large, bright eyes
Deep chest
Strong legs

There is no longer a monarchy in Czechia but Kladrubers are still used to pull carriages by the Danish and Swedish royal families.

HORSE PROFILE
Country: Czechia
Body type: Light **Height:** 15.3–17 hands
Colours: Grey or black
Personality: Noble, calm, strong

HORSE SPORTS

Taking part in a sporty activity with a horse is a great way to build your bond. Whether you just want to have fun or have your eyes set on Olympic Gold, your top priority should always be the welfare of your equine pal. As long as horses are healthy and happy to get involved, they can try all sorts of amazing activities.

SHOWJUMPING AND CROSS-COUNTRY

In showjumping, a horse carries its rider through a course of fences, usually in a time limit. Fences can include upright jumps, crossed poles and spread fences (wider jumps made up of multiple poles). Showjumping horses need to be powerful and precise. Breeds such as the Selle Francais (p51), Holsteiner (p54) and Dutch Warmblood are especially good at it.

If you want a jumping event that's a bit more outdoorsy, try cross-country. This exciting competition takes horses and their riders through a course of natural-looking obstacles, such as log jumps, hedges and ponds.

Eventing is the horsey version of a triathlon. Over the course of several days, horses and their riders take part in three events – dressage, showjumping and cross-country.

DRESSAGE

In dressage, a horse is trained to perform a series of delicate movements, such as pirouettes, loops and elegant trots. Spanish and Portuguese horses and warmblood breeds are traditionally used for dressage, but all horses can try their hoof at it. In recent years, heavier horses and ponies have become popular in the dressage ring.

THE DAILY NEIGH   The Sports Edition

COMBINED DRIVING

In this event, either a single horse, a pair of horses or a team of four pull a light carriage or cart. There are three parts to a combined driving competition: dressage, where particular movements have to be performed; marathon, when the carriage is pulled around a course featuring tunnels, turns and hills; and obstacle driving, when the rider must guide the horses through a narrow set of cones.

In some driving competitions, riders wear smart, old-fashioned clothes.

Good dressage is all about the close bond between the horse and rider. The FEI, the international organisation that oversees horse sports, set rules to ensure that horses are well cared for in training and competitions.

FUN AND GAMES

Want to try something a little more unusual? If you like basketball, give horseball a go – it's a game where teams of players throw a ball to one another while riding horses. Or if gymnastics is more your thing, look up vaulting, a sport where riders perform acrobatics on horseback.

HORSE RACING

Horse racing is one of the most recognisable horse sports but it raises animal welfare issues. Many horses can experience injury and distress during racing. Horse racing is split into three main categories – flat racing, jump racing and harness racing. In flat racing, a horse sprints around a racetrack, while harness racing involves a horse running while pulling a buggy. Jump races, such as hurdles and steeplechases, feature obstacles.

BOERPERD SOUTH AFRICA

BASUTO LESOTHO AND SOUTH AFRICA

Horses were introduced to Egypt in around 1700–1550 BCE. The ancient Egyptians viewed horses as symbols of power – they were used to pull the chariots of pharaohs in peacetime and military figures during battles. Some horses were even mummified and buried alongside their royal owners.

AFRICA

Africa is a continent where speedy stallions thunder over deserts, nimble ponies hike up enormous mountains and hardy horses carry riders across wide savannas. Bred to cope with some of the planet's most extreme climates, Africa's horses are a strong and special herd. The north of Africa is the kingdom of the Barb, an old breed that has influenced many of the continent's home-grown horses, while to the west and east, we meet rare equines, such as the Dongola and M'Bayar. In contrast, the horses in the south reflect the influence of Dutch settlers and the European and Asian breeds they brought with them from the 17th century onwards.

HORSE CULTURE

Horses play a special role in many African cultures. The Hausa people of West Africa, for example, celebrate them in their Kilisa Festival, during which horses wear decorative bridles and saddles and take part in riding displays.

The Mossi people of Burkina Faso also have an ancient tradition of horsemanship. According to legend, the Mossi kingdom was founded by Princess Yennenga, shown above, who ran away from her father's lands on a white horse. She and her son, Ouedraogo (which means 'stallion'), ruled over the Mossi empire. Horse riding and racing remain an important part of Burkina Faso's culture to this day.

AFRICA

BARB

Barbs have been kicking up dust in the North African desert for thousands of years. These speedy horses are riding buddies of the Berber people, the original inhabitants of Morocco, Algeria and Tunisia.

Barbs still play an important role in Berber culture. The horses are used in a dramatic performance called a 'Fantasia', shown here, which celebrates the relationship between horse and rider. During a Fantasia, teams race across the desert before firing an old-fashioned musket (a type of gun) into the air. The team whose performance is the most in sync wins a prize.

Barbs have influenced some of the world's most iconic breeds. When North African armies travelled to Spain in 711 CE, they were accompanied by their trusty Barbs. Spanish breeders admired the power and hardiness of these war horses and used them to create the Andalusian (p60). Later, Barbs played a role in the development of the Thoroughbred (p41), American Quarter Horse (p20) and Argentine Criollo (p30), to name a few.

Short, strong body
Well-defined withers
Narrow, curved (convex) head
Arched neck
Hard feet
Slim but powerful legs

HORSE PROFILE
Country: Morocco, Tunisia and Algeria
Type: Light **Height:** 14.2–15.2 hands
Colours: Grey, bay, chestnut or black
Personality: Tough, agile, gentle

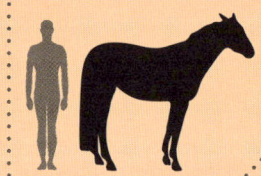

Barbs are distantly related to, and often compared with, Arabs (p88). Like Arabs, Barbs are tough and fast, but they look less elegant and more rustic.

76

DONGOLA

This rare breed is named after the Dongola region of Sudan but it is found in many other West and East African countries, too. Its history is uncertain, but it may have Barb (see opposite), Arab (p88) and Spanish ancestry. As there are no official breeding programmes for Dongolas, the look and size of these horses varies between countries.

The Dongola has a particularly special relationship with the Fulani people of Cameroon. The Fulani cherish their horses, and Dongolas appear in parades and ceremonies, as well as being used for general riding.

Large, proud head with a convex (curved) profile

Flat croup (rump)

Long back

Usually has white markings on head and lower legs

Slender legs

HORSE PROFILE
Country: Sudan, Cameroon and Eritrea **Type:** Light
Height: 15–15.2 hands
Colours: Black, chestnut or bay
Personality: Energetic, spirited, strong

BHIRUM

This handsome pony was developed in the north of Nigeria in West Africa. Bhirums are thought to be related to Barbs (see opposite) and a very rare (possibly extinct) Cameroonian breed called the Poney Mousseye.

These little horses have tough, quiet personalities – they don't neigh very much, preferring to get on calmly with their work. In Nigeria, Bhirum ponies are used for light draught and pack jobs, as well as for general riding.

Small head with alert ears

Short neck

Compact pony with horse-like proportions

Deep chest

Strong legs

HORSE PROFILE
Country: Nigeria
Type: Pony **Height:** 14–14.2 hands
Colours: Various solid colours, including black, bay, chestnut or grey
Personality: Reliable, gentle, hard-working

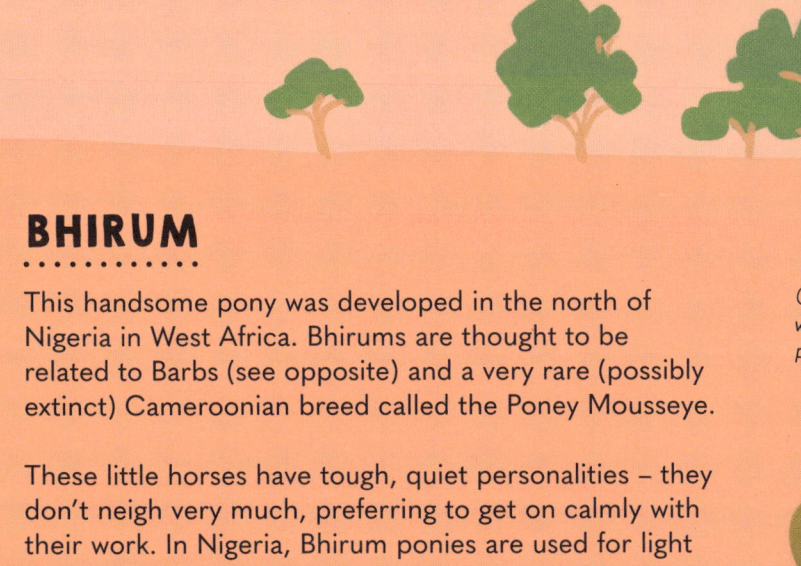

AFRICA

M'BAYAR

The M'Bayar is a sturdy pony that is thought to have been developed from the Barb (p76) in the region of Baol in central Senegal. In ancient times, this area was renowned for its strong, speedy horses, which were traded with neighbouring kingdoms. The M'Bayar is especially prized for its adaptable and willing temperament.

Stocky body
Short neck
Broad chest
Long, strong legs

HORSE PROFILE
Country: Senegal
Type: Pony **Height:** 13–14 hands
Colours: Usually bay or chestnut
Personality: Calm, strong, hard-working

Horses and ponies play an essential role in Senegalese life. Millions of people in Senegal rely on equines like M'Bayars, to help them farm the land and for transport.

FLEUVE

The exact origins of this slender breed are unknown, but it's thought the Fleuve was created by crossing Barbs (p76) with local ponies. Its name comes from the French word for 'river' and it suits this breed well – like a river, Fleuves are swift and powerful.

Fleuves used to belong to Senegalese chieftains. Today, they are used for riding and horse racing, which is a popular sport in Senegal.

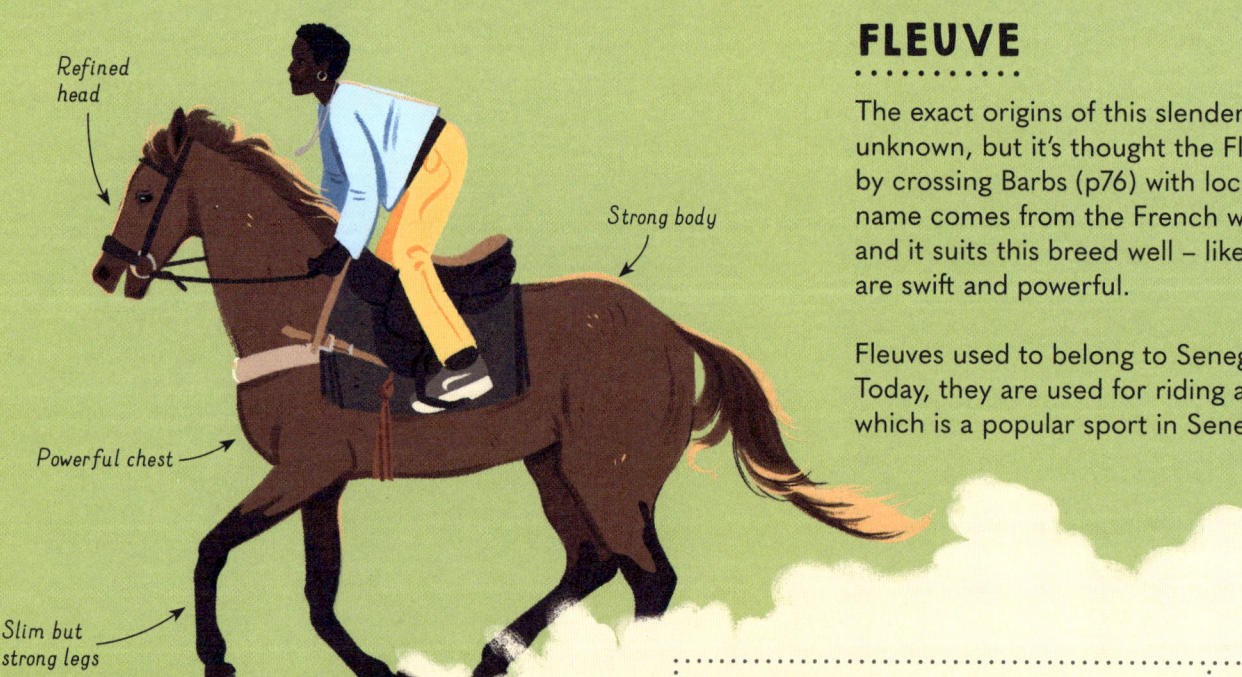

Refined head
Strong body
Powerful chest
Slim but strong legs

HORSE PROFILE
Country: Senegal **Type:** Light
Height: Usually around 14 hands
Colours: Often grey, but can be brown or bay
Personality: Energetic, speedy, hardy

BASUTO

The Basuto has its roots in Arab (p88) and Middle Eastern horses that were brought to South Africa in the 1650s by Dutch settlers (called Boers). These horses were used to create two breeds – the larger Cape Horse and the smaller, stockier Basuto. The Cape Horse is now extinct, but the Basuto has survived.

Basutos were developed by Dutch breeders in the mountains of South Africa and Lesotho. These sure-footed ponies are fantastic climbers, and are used to carrying farmers and tourists over steep, rocky terrain. Thanks to their long strides, they are very comfortable to ride.

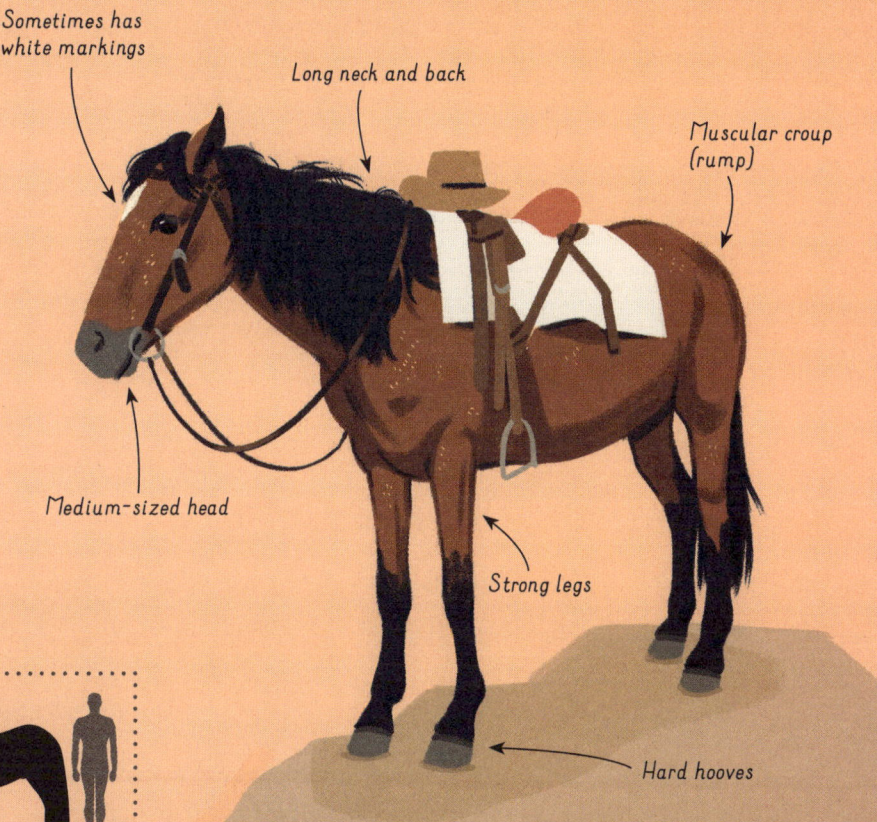

Sometimes has white markings
Long neck and back
Muscular croup (rump)
Medium-sized head
Strong legs
Hard hooves

HORSE PROFILE
Country: Lesotho and South Africa
Type: Pony **Height:** 14.2 hands
Colours: Chestnut, grey, brown, black or bay
Personality: Hardy, courageous, friendly

BOERPERD

The Boerperd is a descendant of the Cape Horse (see above) and was named after the Dutch settlers who developed it in the 19th century. They mixed Cape Horses with British breeds, including Thoroughbreds (p41), Cleveland Bays and Hackneys (p41), to create tough horses with great stamina and speed.

Boerperds were used as war horses in the Second Boer War (1899–1902) and the breed almost died out as a result. Six herds survived and were used to redevelop the breed between the 1940s and 1990s. Today, Boerperds are used for sports such as eventing and dressage, and for riding safari holidays in South Africa.

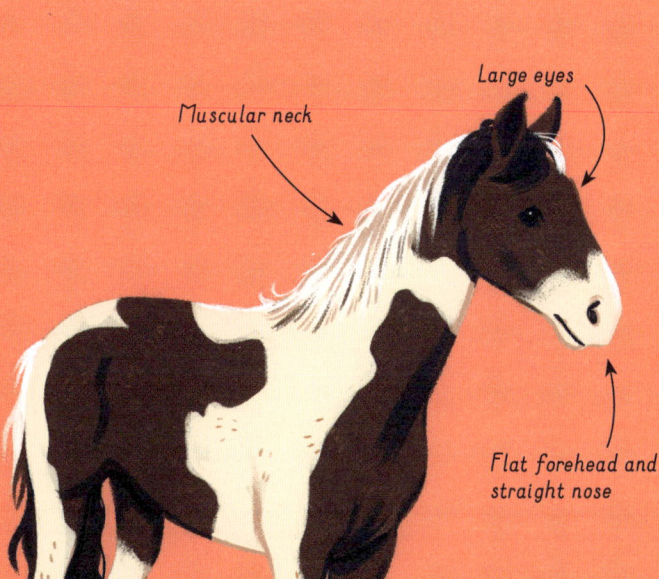

Muscular neck
Large eyes
Flat forehead and straight nose
Strong legs
Hard hooves

HORSE PROFILE
Country: South Africa
Type: Light **Height:** 14–16 hands
Colours: Various colours, including black, dun, chestnut, palomino or pinto
Personality: Strong, trustworthy, brave

WILD HORSES

All of the horse breeds in this book belong to one species, *Equus caballus,* or the domestic horse. But there are seven other species of horse living in the world today. One of these is the domestic donkey (pp34–35). The other six live in the wild. Let's meet them!

African wild asses are divided into two subspecies – the Nubian wild ass and the Somali wild ass. You can tell them apart because the Somali wild ass has zebra-like stripes on its legs.

ZEBRAS

There are three species of zebra: the mountain zebra, the plains zebra and the Grévy's zebra. They are found in savanna, scrubland and mountainous regions in eastern and southern Africa. Plains and mountain zebra live in family groups called harems, led by a dominant male, while Grévy's zebra usually live alone or in loose herds.

Every individual zebra has a pattern of stripes that is completely unique – just like your fingerprints are to you. Scientists think that a zebra's stripes may help to deter horse flies, which can spread disease among horses. It's thought that the stripes confuse the flies, preventing them from biting the zebra.

AFRICAN WILD ASS

Found in the deserts and grasslands of Eritrea, Ethiopia and Somalia, the African wild ass is a critically endangered member of the horse family. There are thought to be fewer than 600 alive in the wild today.

This tough equine is the ancestor of the domestic donkey, and the two species look very similar. Like donkeys, African wild asses have big ears, a stiff mane and a tufted tail. They also make a loud hee-haw sound, which travels easily across the open desert when the animals need to communicate with each other. Although females and their young sometimes form herds, African wild asses live alone or in casual groups for most of their lives.

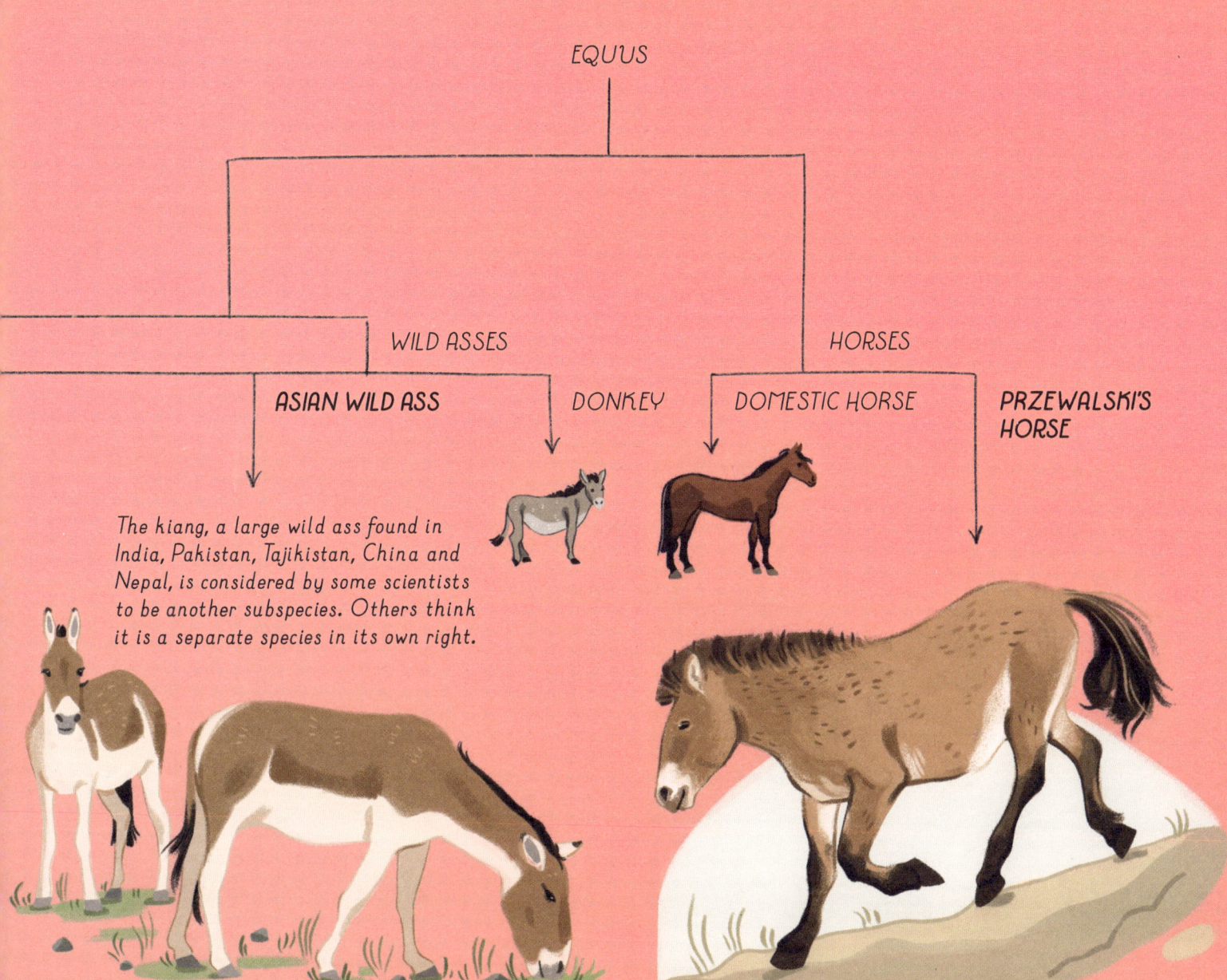

ASIAN WILD ASS

Also known as the onager, the Asian wild ass is made up of four living subspecies: the Turkmenian kulan, Persian onager, Mongolian wild ass and Indian wild ass. All are endangered due to poaching, drought and catching diseases from farm animals.

Asian wild asses live in loose family groups and in extreme environments, roaming deserts, steppes and mountains across Asia. They look more horse-like than their African relatives, with longer legs, larger bodies and shorter ears. Before donkeys were developed, onagers were tamed in ancient times and trained to pull carts and ploughs.

PRZEWALSKI'S HORSE

The Przewalski's horse (you say it 'sheh-VAHL-skee') is a distant cousin of the domestic horse. With their stocky bodies and a thick, brush-like manes, Przewalski's are perfectly adapted to a tough life on the windswept steppes and deserts of eastern Asia.

The species was named after a Russian explorer who encountered herds on his travels in the 1870s. Less than 100 years later, the horses were declared extinct in the wild. Breeding programmes have reintroduced Przewalski's horses to their original habitats in Mongolia, China and Russia, but they are still endangered, with only around 2,000 living in the wild today.

1. **ORLOV TROTTER** – RUSSIA
2. **DON** – RUSSIA
3. **VLADIMIR** – RUSSIA
4. **KABARDIN** – RUSSIA
5. **BUDYONNY** – RUSSIA
6. **TERSK** – RUSSIA
7. **ARAB** – BAHRAIN, IRAN, IRAQ, KUWAIT, OMAN, QATAR, SAUDI ARABIA, UAE, YEMEN
8. **CASPIAN** – IRAN
9. **AKHAL-TEKE** – TURKMENISTAN
10. **KARABAKH** – AZERBAIJAN
11. **KARABAIR** – UZBEKISTAN AND TURKMENISTAN
12. **LOKAI** – TAJIKISTAN
13. **MONGOLIAN HORSE** – MONGOLIA AND CHINA
14. **MARWARI** – INDIA
15. **KATHIAWARI** – INDIA
16. **SPITI** – INDIA
17. **SUMBA** – INDONESIA
18. **SANDALWOOD** – INDONESIA
19. **TIMOR** – INDONESIAA
20. **BATAK** – INDONESIA
21. **JAVA** – INDONESIA
22. **KISO** – JAPAN
23. **HOKKAIDO** – JAPAN
24. **TOKARA** – JAPAN

Orlov Trotters have an especially fast trot. Their combination of power and speed made them popular for harness racing in the 19th century.

ASIA

Asia is the original home of the horse. It was here that wild horses were first tamed around 4000 BCE. Ever since, the continent's equines have been shaped by its varied cultures and geography. This is a land of desert-dwelling athletes like the Arab, mighty mountaineers such as the Spiti, and regal Russian trotters. Because they have developed in extreme environments, many Asian breeds are small and stocky equines. But don't let their size fool you. These are some of the toughest ponies around.

THE LAND OF THE HORSE

Horses have been cherished by the people of Mongolia for thousands of years. Many Mongolians are semi-nomadic, meaning they move from one location to another as the seasons change. Horses are essential to this way of life, acting as the main mode of transport. In the Mongolian countryside, children learn to ride as young as three years old!

Horses are also used for herding and sport. The country's native breed, the Mongolian Horse, is traditionally ridden by eagle hunters – Kazakh people who use tame golden eagles to hunt in Mongolia's rugged mountains.

A Kabardin puts on fat much more quickly than most other horses. This adaptation originally helped the horse to survive cold Russian winters. If a Kabardin lives in a warmer climate, it needs a lot of daily exercise to make sure it stays a healthy weight.

In Hinduism, Uchchaihshravas is the king of all horses. He has a pure-white coat and seven heads. Uchchaihshravas appears during a struggle between Hindu gods and demons called the Churning of the Milk Ocean.

83

ASIA

ORLOV TROTTER

Imagine it is a winter's night in 19th-century Russia and you have been invited to a grand ball. There's only one horse that is strong enough to pull your sleigh over icy roads, battle through blizzards, and get you to the party with speed and style – the Orlov Trotter.

This noble-looking breed was developed by a Russian nobleman, Count Alexei Orlov, in the 1770s by crossing Arab (p88) stallions with European mares. Throughout the 19th century, Orlov Trotters were used to transport emperors and aristocrats across Russia. The breed declined after the Russian Revolution in 1917, when the royal family's rule came to an end, but Orlov Trotters are still celebrated today as a symbol of the country's culture.

Orlov Trotters are traditionally used in troikas – a type of Russian harness where three horses stand alongside one another to pull a carriage or sleigh. The horse in the middle is the strongest and maintains a steady trot, while the horses on either side canter. Their combined power means a team of horses in a troika can maintain speeds of around 50 km (30 miles) per hour over long distances.

Big eyes
Elegant, arched neck
Large head
Big, muscular body
Powerful legs

HORSE PROFILE
Country: Russia
Type: Light **Height:** 15.2–17 hands
Colours: Usually grey, but can also be black, bay or chestnut
Personality: Elegant, fast, hard-working

Orlov Trotters have an especially fast trot. Their combination of power and speed made them popular for harness racing in the 19th century.

DON

This rustic horse is named after the River Don, which flows through the steppes (grasslands) in the south of Russia. Centuries ago, this landscape was home to tough, semi-wild horses. It was also home to a group of people called the Cossacks, like the rider shown in this image, who were renowned for their horse-riding and battle skills.

The Cossacks mixed the local horses with other Asian breeds to create incredibly hardy equines for their soldiers. In the 19th century, Dons were crossed with Orlov Trotters (see opposite) and Thoroughbreds (p41) to make the breed larger and more refined. Dons were used by the Russian army up until the 1950s, and today they make robust cross-country and general-riding horses.

Straight neck
Large nostrils
Big, bold eyes
Long back
Muscular chest
Long, sturdy legs

HORSE PROFILE
Country: Russia **Type:** Light
Height: 15.1–15.3 hands
Colours: Usually chestnut, but can be bay, black or grey too
Personality: Hardy, athletic, even-tempered

VLADIMIR

Russia didn't have its own breed of heavy horse until the early 20th century, when the Vladimir was developed. Farmers in the countryside northeast of Moscow crossed various draught breeds, including Percherons (p50), Suffolk Punches (p46), Clydesdales (p38) and Shires (p40), to create this strong and reliable horse. It was officially recognised as a breed in 1946.

The Vladimir is an easy-going breed that can help out with all sorts of pulling and carrying jobs on the farm. It also has a very energetic trot, making it well suited for pulling a special type of Russian harness called a troika (see opposite).

Long head with convex (curved) nose
Long back and broad chest
Kindly expression
Muscular neck
Usually has feathering around feet
Often has white markings on legs and face

HORSE PROFILE
Country: Russia **Type:** Heavy
Height: 15.5–15.8 hands
Colours: Usually bay
Personality: Powerful, energetic, good-tempered

ASIA

KABARDIN

If you fancy an adventurous hack, take a Kabardin for a ride. For at least 400 years, Kabardins have been bred by tribespeople in the Caucasus Mountains that straddle Russia, Georgia and Azerbaijan. These horses have exceptionally strong lungs and hearts to cope with the lack of oxygen at high altitudes, and an uncanny ability to pick their way down mountain paths in the darkest of nights and wildest of weathers.

Their ancestors are thought to have been a mix of Turkoman (an old Asian breed), Arab (p88) and Karabakh (p90) horses. Historically, farmers grazed herds of Kabardins in high mountain pastures during the summer and brought them down to the foothills for the winter – a tradition that continues today in some rural areas.

Kabardins were used on hill farms for light work, such as pulling hay carts during the harvest, and by armies to cross mountains in times of war. Over the centuries, they have also been used to strengthen other breeds due to their natural hardiness.

- Flowing mane and tail
- Short, solid back
- Straight shoulders
- Alert ears
- Bright, expressive eyes
- Very hard hooves (these horses never need shoes)

HORSE PROFILE
Country: Russia **Type:** Light
Height: 14.1–15.1 hands
Colours: Bay, black or grey
Personality: Agile, strong, sociable

BUDYONNY

The Budyonny was developed by (and named after) a Russian horse breeder and army commander called Semyon Budyonny between the 1920s and 1940s. Budyonny wanted to create a new breed to boost his country's horse population following World War I (1914–1918) and the Russian Revolution (1917–1923). He crossed Dons (p85) with Thoroughbreds (p41) and another Russian breed called a Chernomor – a mountain horse renowned for its stamina and toughness.

Originally used as military riding horses, Budyonnys were bred to be courageous, light on their feet and smooth to ride. Today, they make great dressage, showjumping and eventing horses.

HORSE PROFILE
Country: Russia **Type:** Light
Height: 16–16.1 hands
Colours: Typically chestnut, but can be bay, grey, brown or black
Personality: Energetic, brave, intelligent

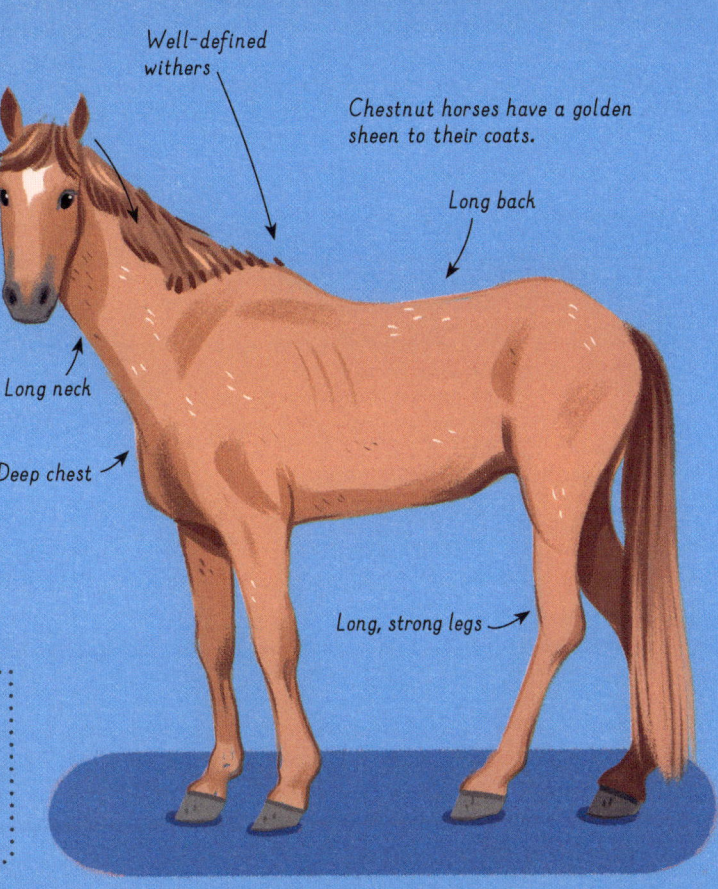

Well-defined withers
Chestnut horses have a golden sheen to their coats.
Long back
Long neck
Deep chest
Long, strong legs

TERSK

Step right up and meet one of the greatest showmen of the horse world. Tersks are born performers and are often ridden by acrobats in Russian circuses, as shown here. They are also popular in showjumping, dressage and eventing.

Like the Budyonny, the Tersk was developed between the 1920s and 1940s in the aftermath of World War I and the Russian Revolution. At a farm in the Caucasus Mountains in the south-west of Russia, Arab horses were mixed with Don (p85), Kabardin (see opposite) and a now-extinct Ukrainian breed called a Stretlet to make this nimble riding horse.

Handsome head with expressive eyes
Long shoulders
Broad, strong back
Silky mane and tail
Deep chest
Elegant legs

HORSE PROFILE
Country: Russia **Type:** Light
Height: 15 hands
Colours: Usually grey or white
Personality: Clever, gentle, sure-footed

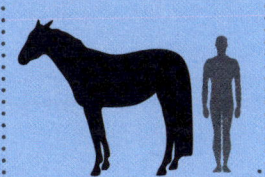

ASIA

ARAB

The Arab is one of the world's oldest and most influential breeds. The history of these beautiful horses can be traced to at least 3000 BCE.

They were developed on the Arabian Peninsula by the desert-dwelling Bedouin people as stealthy war horses. To survive the blistering temperatures and lack of water, Bedouin horses had to be exceptionally tough. The horses lived closely alongside their owners – sometimes sleeping inside their family's tent at night to prevent them from being stolen – so a compact build and gentle disposition was also essential.

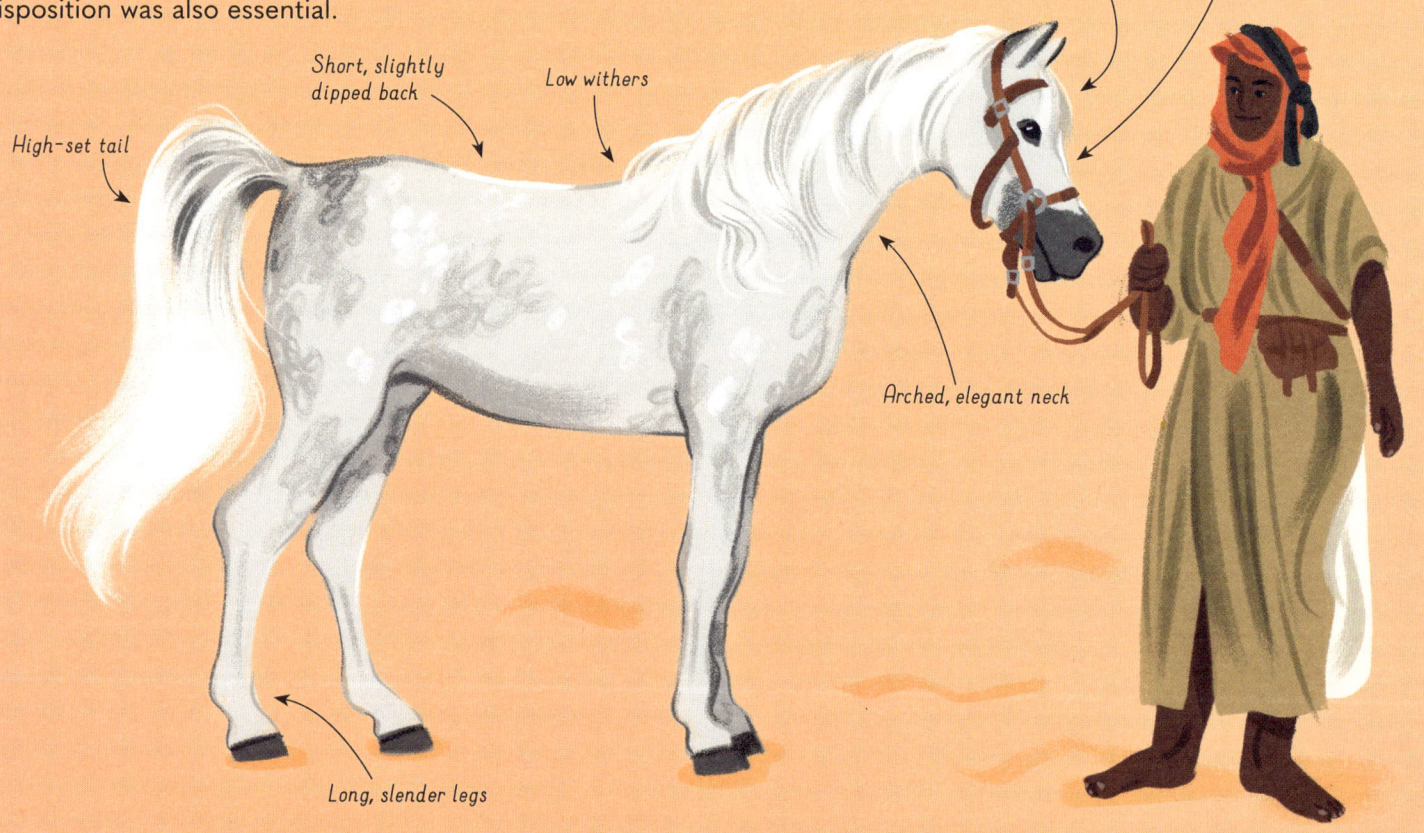

- Large, expressive eyes
- A slightly dished (curved) face
- Short, slightly dipped back
- Low withers
- High-set tail
- Arched, elegant neck
- Long, slender legs

Arab horses were introduced to Europe from the 8th century onwards, and they played a key role in the development of many modern breeds – most famously, the Thoroughbred (p41). Although they are now found all over the world, Arabs remain true to their desert roots. Combining speed, stamina, agility and hardiness, they excel in most horsey activities, from showjumping and dressage to endurance racing and ranch work.

HORSE PROFILE
Country: Bahrain, Iran, Iraq, Kuwait, Oman, Qatar, Saudi Arabia, UAE and Yemen
Type: Light **Height:** 14.2–15.3 hands
Colours: Bay, grey, chestnut, black or roan
Personality: Fiery, intelligent, courageous

CASPIAN

In ancient Persia (c.550–330 BCE), these little horses were kept for chariot racing and as royal pets. But when the Persian Empire ended, its precious horses disappeared ... or so it seemed. A small population survived in Iran's Alborz Mountains on the shores of the Caspian Sea, where they were used by local people for transport and carrying goods.

In the 1960s, Louise Firouz, an American living in Iran, came in search of small horses for her riding school. She was struck by the Caspian's story, and devoted the rest of her life to conserving the breed. Caspians make brilliant children's horses due to their dainty size, easy movements and kind characters.

HORSE PROFILE
Country: Iran
Type: Pony **Height:** 11.2–12.2 hands
Colours: All colours except skewbald or piebald
Personality: Gentle, athletic, willing

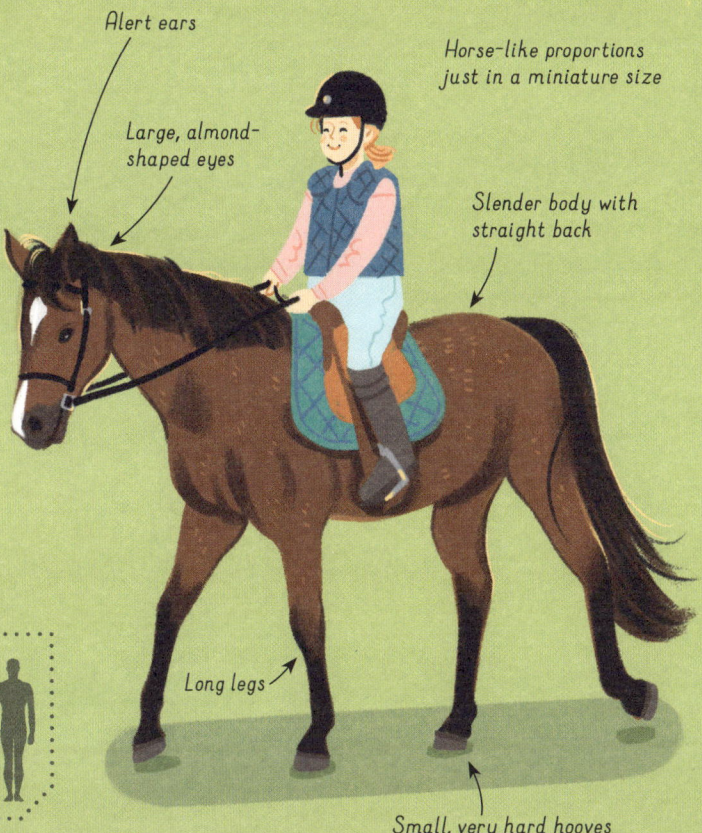

- Alert ears
- Horse-like proportions just in a miniature size
- Large, almond-shaped eyes
- Slender body with straight back
- Long legs
- Small, very hard hooves

AKHAL-TEKE

These one-of-a-kind horses come from the Karakum Desert in modern-day Turkmenistan. They were developed at least 3,000 years ago by the nomadic Teke people to carry riders over the vast, dusty landscape. Akhal-Tekes can go for days with little water, run effortlessly across the dunes, and have coats that shimmer like gold in the sun.

Traditionally, these horses spent their days covering long distances in the heat and their nights tethered to their rider's tent. As result, Akhal-Tekes form intense, dog-like bonds with their owners – sometimes even nipping strangers who they see as a threat to their beloved person!

HORSE PROFILE
Country: Turkmenistan
Type: Light **Height:** 14–16 hands
Colours: Often dun, but can be bay, chestnut, black, grey or silver
Personality: Devoted, intelligent, athletic

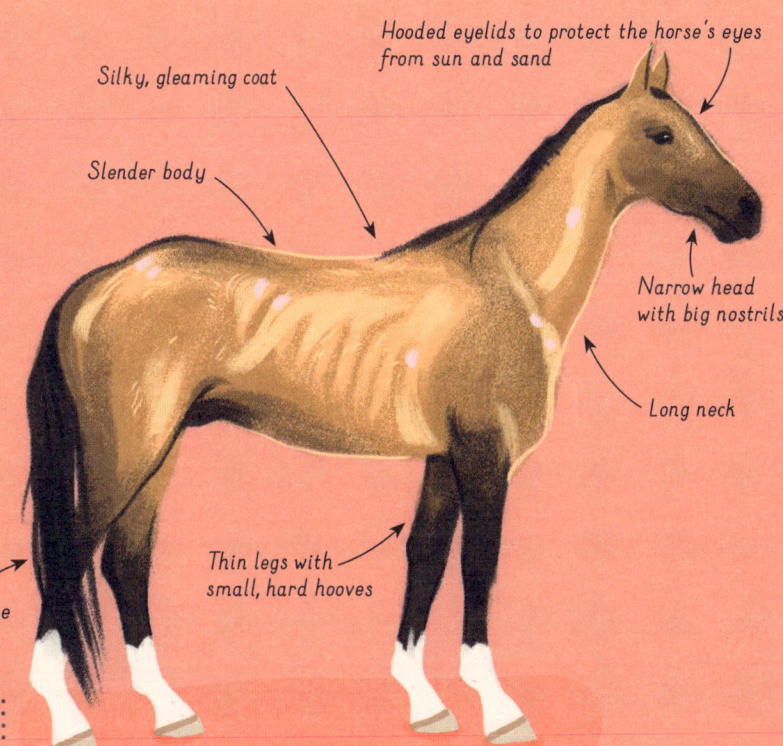

- Hooded eyelids to protect the horse's eyes from sun and sand
- Silky, gleaming coat
- Slender body
- Narrow head with big nostrils
- Long neck
- Fine mane and tail
- Thin legs with small, hard hooves

An Akhal-Teke's coat hairs have a special structure, which means that sunlight bends as it passes through each individual hair. This gives the horse's coat its magical glimmer.

ASIA

KARABAKH

The Karabakh is named after a region of Azerbaijan where it has been used as a riding and racing horse for hundreds of years. An adaptable breed, the Karabakh is just as comfortable trotting up treacherous mountain paths as it is galloping across windswept steppes (grasslands).

Although the breed is prized in its homeland and is Azerbaijan's national animal, there are only around 1,000 Karabakhs alive today. These are used in several Azerbaijani horse-riding sports.

HORSE PROFILE
Country: Azerbaijan
Type: Light **Height:** 14–15 hands
Colours: Chestnut, bay or dun
Personality: Calm, agile, tough

Coat usually has a golden tint
Small head with alert eyes and ears
Compact, muscular body
Deep chest
Hard hooves

This horse is taking part in the traditional sport of chovgan. A bit like polo, it involves two teams trying to hit a ball into their opponent's goal using wooden mallets.

KARABAIR

One thousand years ago, the area of Central Asia that is now Uzbekistan and Tajikistan sat on ancient trade routes. Desert breeds, such as Arabs (p88), were sold along these routes and some were eventually crossed with local horses to create the fast and fiery Karabair.

For centuries, this breed has been used to play a dramatic sport called *uloq*, in which teams of riders have to carry a goat carcass to their opponent's goal. In Uzbekistan, the game is played on enormous plains, requiring great stamina and agility from the horses.

Medium-sized head with straight profile
Short, wide back
Muscular neck
Shallow chest
Strong, slender legs
Very hard hooves

HORSE PROFILE
Country: Uzbekistan and Tajikistan
Type: Light **Height:** 14.3–15.2 hands
Colours: Usually bay, chestnut, black or grey
Personality: Athletic, robust, courageous

LOKAI

The Lokai was developed in the 16th century by tribespeople living in the Pamir Mountains in modern-day Tajikistan. Breeders mixed local horses with various Asian breeds, including Karabairs (see opposite) and Akhal-Tekes (p89), and later Arabs (p88), Tersks (p87) and Thoroughbreds (p41). The result was a fearless and nimble horse that could carry riders up the steepest of paths.

The Pamirs is a remote landscape of rocky plains, glaciers and high snow-capped peaks. With few roads, Lokais are the main means of transport for people here. These tough horses are also used for uloq (see opposite).

HORSE PROFILE
Country: Tajikistan
Type: Light **Height:** 14–15 hands
Colours: Usually bay, grey or chestnut
Personality: Hardy, sure-footed, loyal

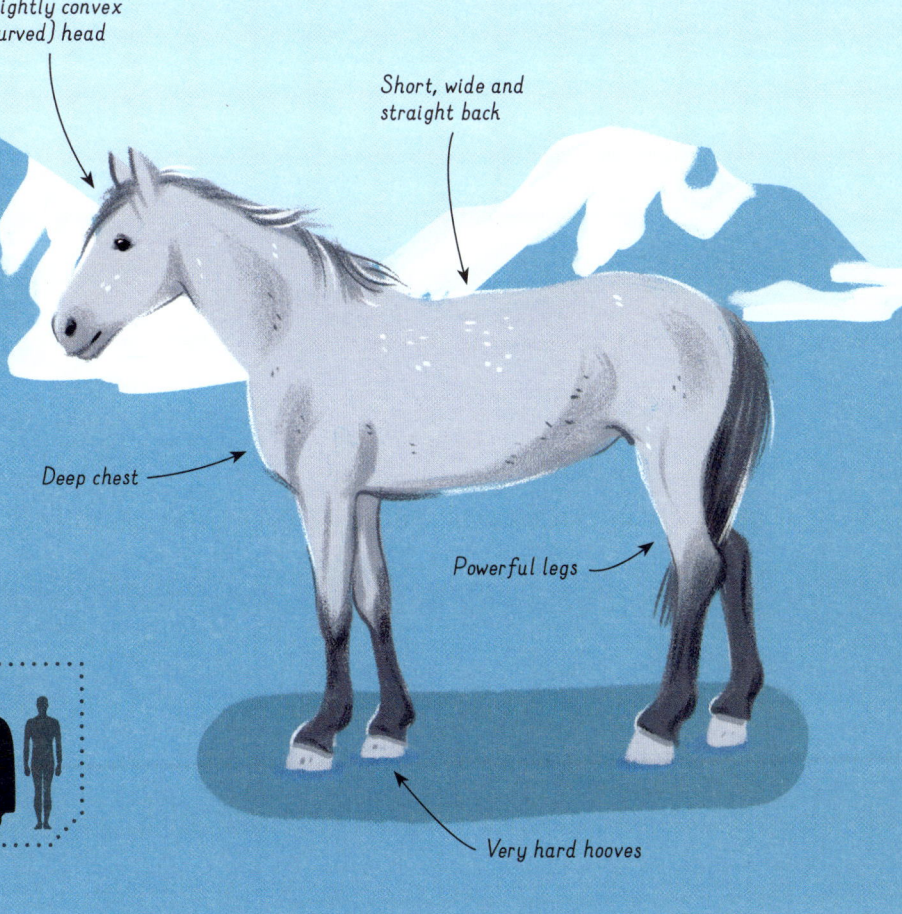

Slightly convex (curved) head
Short, wide and straight back
Deep chest
Powerful legs
Very hard hooves

MONGOLIAN HORSE

These immensely hardy horses (despite being pony-size, they are always called horses) have lived semi-wild on the Mongolian steppes for centuries. They stay outside all year round, foraging for their own food and surviving in extreme conditions – temperatures can fall to -40°C (-40°F) in the country during the winter months.

Their ancestors were ridden by the armies of Genghis Khan, the fierce leader of the Mongol Empire, in the 13th century and it's thought the breed has hardly changed since. These horses are still central to the culture of Mongolia's nomadic peoples, who use them for riding, transport, hunting and epic long-distance races.

Grows a thick coat in winter
Large head with intelligent expression
Shaggy mane and tail
Hairy
Compact, muscly body
Short but powerful legs
Hard, strong hooves

The milk of Mongolian mares is used to produce kumis, a popular drink in Mongolia, while the thick hairs of the horse's tails are used to make rope and violin strings.

HORSE PROFILE
Country: Mongolia and China
Type: Pony **Height:** 12–14 hands
Colours: Various colours, including dun, black, bay or white
Personality: Independent, powerful, tough

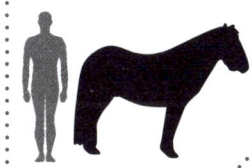

HOW TO SPEAK HORSE

If you haven't spent much time with horses and ponies before, they can seem like intimidating and hard-to-read animals. But they actually send very clear messages with their bodies to tell us how they're feeling. Learning how to read a horse or pony's body language, and understanding when they're happy, want attention or need space, means you can have the best possible relationship with your horsey pal.

HORSE HELLOS

Think about how you say hello to another person – you'd usually hug, wave or maybe shake hands if you don't know them very well. Greetings are just as important to horses. Here's how to say hi to a horse:

• Ask permission from the horse's owner before you approach it. If the owner is happy for you to say hello, walk slowly and confidently towards the horse.

• Always greet a horse from the front where it can see you. Even if you know a horse, you should never approach a horse from behind as they are powerful animals that can kick if they feel frightened.

• Speak softly and calmy – horses prefer low-pitched sounds.

• Study the horse's body language to make sure it's feeling happy and relaxed. Read the rest of this page to learn what to look out for.

• If the horse seems happy, hold out your hand so it can smell you. If a horse is ready for you to stroke it, it will usually lightly touch your hand with its nose. If the horse turns away, it probably doesn't want to be petted right now. Respect this and let it be.

A HAPPY HORSE

A happy horse gives off chilled-out vibes. Its ears are pricked up in an attentive position. Its eyes are open and looking brightly at you. The horse's muzzle looks relaxed and its mouth is closed. A happy horse may be resting one of its back legs by holding its hoof slightly off the ground. It's safe to hold out a hand to see if this horse would like to say hi to you.

A RESTING HORSE

A sleepy horse will look even more relaxed. Its eyes are half closed, its ears are pointed slightly to the side and its lower lip may be drooping a little as it dozes. The horse may be resting a back leg and bending its head down. Make sure you approach a sleepy horse carefully (from the front) to avoid startling it.

A WORRIED HORSE

An anxious horse has its ears pointing backwards. Its face looks tense, with the muscles above its eyes making a worried 'V' shape. It may be making a chewing movement with its mouth, too. This sort of behaviour suggests the horse is stressed – it may not know you well, so feels uncertain about you approaching. Move away to give this horse some space, so it understands you aren't a threat.

AN UNHAPPY HORSE

An angry or frightened horse makes its feelings clear. Its ears are flattened backwards, its teeth are bared and it's stomping its hooves. This horse is saying, 'Back off, or I will bite!' When a horse is this unhappy, you can usually see the whites of its eyes. It may be angrily swishing its tail, sweating and visibly shaking. Stop whatever you're doing and stay away from this horse.

NEIGH-CE TO MEET YOU!

Horses also use sounds to express how they're feeling. There are four types of horsey noises: whinnies (or neighs), nickers, snorts and squeals. A whinny is a loud, high-pitched neigh. Horses use this sound to call to one another, usually over long distances. A nicker is a low, purring sound. Horses use nickers to say, 'Come to me,' – for instance, when a mare is calling back her foal, or when a horse sees their favourite human approaching with some tasty hay. Snorts express alarm, while high-pitched squeals are used to communicate aggression.

ASIA

MARWARI

Once you've met a Marwari you will never forget it – just look at those curly ears! These elegant equines were originally bred as war horses in the Thar Desert in north-west India from the 12th century.

With a Marwari, a warrior didn't need to worry about getting lost in the dizzying landscape of sand dunes. Marwaris have a heightened sense of smell and hearing, as well as a legendary homing instinct, meaning they'd always get their rider back to camp safely.

By the 1940s, the number of Marwari had fallen, so fans of the breed, including a Maharaja (prince) called Umaid Singhji, established breeding programmes to save them. Today, these noble horses are used for weddings and religious festivals in India, as well as for desert riding safaris.

Ears that curve inwards so the tips touch

Slim, sleek body with strong back

Slope from croup (rump) to tail

Thin skin to cope with hot temperatures in the desert

Long legs

Very hard hooves

HORSE PROFILE
Country: India
Type: Light **Height:** 14–16 hands
Colours: Various colours, including bay, grey, chestnut, palomino or skewbald
Personality: Loyal, brave, elegant

Marwaris have a natural four-beat gait called a revaal or rehwal, which allows the horse to carry its rider smoothly and quickly over tough terrain and long distances.

KATHIAWARI

The Kathiawari is the Marwari's stockier relative. It was developed in the 16th century by Indian royals in the Kathiawar peninsula in west India. They were bred as hardy war horses, capable of carrying soldiers through the hot, desert landscape and able to survive on limited food.

Today, these sensible horses are used for leisure riding and by police forces in India. They are also used for a fast-paced horsey sport called tent-pegging where a rider uses a sword or lance to pick up a target from the ground while galloping.

Inward-curving ears, which touch and sometimes overlap at the tips

Large, intelligent eyes

Small head with short muzzle and big nostrils

Stocky, muscular body – shorter than the Marwari

Round hooves

HORSE PROFILE
Country: India
Type: Light **Height:** 14–15 hands
Colours: Usually chestnut, but can also be bay, grey or dun
Personality: Agile, courageous, affectionate

SPITI

The Spiti (also known as the Chamurthi) is only found in a remote valley in the Himalaya Mountains in northern India. Spiti move with ease along icy paths and work comfortably at high altitudes. As a result, they are used for all sorts of jobs, from transporting food and logs to helping farmers carry lambs to meadows in the spring (shown here).

Herds of Spiti are left to roam freely in the valley during summer. Because snow leopards prowl the surrounding slopes, villagers take it in turns to watch over the ponies and bring them indoors in winter.

Short, strong back

Long, thick mane and tail

Barrel-shaped body

Thick legs

Hard, round hooves

HORSE PROFILE
Country: India
Type: Pony **Height:** 9–12 hands
Colours: Various colours, including grey, black, brown or bay
Personality: Strong, reliable, easy-going

ASIA

SUMBA

Named after the tropical island of Sumba, this tough, agile pony is thought to be descended from Mongolian and Chinese horses, which were brought to the island by traders and travellers in the 14th century. As well as carrying crops and tourists, the ponies feature in dance festivals on the island, where they wear bells around their legs. Guided by their riders, the ponies move in time to a drumbeat.

HORSE PROFILE
Country: Indonesia
Type: Pony **Height:** 12–12.2 hands
Colours: All solid colours but usually dun
Personality: Tough, athletic, nimble

SANDALWOOD

The Sandalwood is named after a fragrant tree that has been an important trade item on Sumba for centuries. The breed was developed from Mongolian and Arab (p88) horses. Sumba holds a horse festival each year to celebrate this special breed – the ponies wear decorative bridles and compete in riding competitions. The rest of the time, many enjoy swimming in the island's bright blue waters!

HORSE PROFILE
Country: Indonesia
Type: Pony **Height:** 13.1 hands
Colours: Any solid colour
Personality: Friendly, fast, tough

TIMOR

Like rough diamonds, these ponies are small, rare and exceptionally tough. No one is quite sure how long ponies have been on the island of Timor, but it's thought they were introduced by traders from the 6th or 7th century onwards. Local people use Timors for racing, and farm and cattle work.

HORSE PROFILE
Country: Indonesia
Type: Pony **Height:** 10–12 hands
Colours: Brown, black, bay or grey
Personality: Strong, hardy, hard-working

BATAK

The hardy Batak was developed by and named after the Batak people who live on the island of Sumatra. They are mainly bred for riding, transporting goods and racing. Because they are so healthy, Bataks are often used to improve other local breeds as well.

HORSE PROFILE
Country: Indonesia
Type: Pony **Height:** 13 hands
Colours: All solid colours
Personality: Spirited, friendly, strong

JAVA

This pony's ancestors were brought to the tropical island of Java by traders from the 7th century onwards. Javas are prized for their hard-working natures. They help farmers collect crops, such as tea and sugar; transport goods and people through the island's cities; and are used for tourist treks to the island's natural wonders.

HORSE PROFILE
Country: Indonesia
Type: Pony **Height:** 11.2–12.2 hands
Colours: Any colour
Personality: Hardy, sure-footed, kind-natured

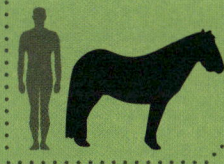

ASIA

KISO

Japan's famous samurai were powerful warriors and skilled horse-riders who helped rule the country from the 12th to 19th centuries. These fearsome fighters favoured one breed in particular – the Kiso. At first glance, these small ponies seem an unusual choice, but they have a brave heart and a noble character to match that of any samurai.

Long before it caught the attention of the samurai, the Kiso was used as a sturdy farm pony in the peaceful forests of the Kiso Valley on Japan's main island, Honshu. Hard-working and gentle, the ponies were treated as part of the family and often lived under the same roof as their owners.

Despite its impressive history, the Kiso almost died out in the 1930s. Although fans set up a conservation project to save the breed, only a few hundred are alive today. You can meet these special ponies at rare-breed centres in Japan, where they are used for trekking and therapy riding.

Thick mane and tail

Strong hooves

Round tummy

Short, sturdy legs

Short neck

Large head with big, gentle eyes

HORSE PROFILE
Country: Japan
Type: Pony Height: 13 hands
Colours: Usually bay
Personality: Loyal, strong, kind-natured

Kiso are still used for a traditional samurai sport called yabusame, where a rider on a galloping horse fires arrows at a target.

HOKKAIDO

Hokkaido ponies (also known as Dosanko) come from the mountainous island of Hokkaido in the far north of Japan. In the 15th century, fisherman from Honshu took horses to the island each spring to help them haul cartloads of herring during the fish harvest.

Compact body · *Neat head* · *Grows a thick coat in winter* · *Round feet with light feathering* · *Slim but muscular legs*

HORSE PROFILE
Country: Japan
Type: Pony **Height:** 13–13.2 hands
Colours: Various colours but often roan
Personality: Resourceful, strong, gentle

At the end of the season, the horses were left behind to fend for themselves and they developed into a strong and resourceful breed. In the past, the ponies were used for farm work and transporting goods. Today, you're more likely to see them carrying tourists or pulling sleds through the island's snowy mountains.

TOKARA

This extremely rare pony comes from a group of remote islands in the south of Japan. Little was known about the Tokara until the 1950s, when a Japanese professor travelled to the islands and encountered a herd.

It's thought the ancestors of these hardy ponies were brought to the islands in the late 19th century and used by local people for transport and to work on sugarcane farms. Today, the breed is celebrated as a 'natural monument', reflecting the Tokara's important role in the region's farming history.

Strong neck · *Delicate head* · *Thick mane and tail* · *Round body* · *Short legs* · *Hard hooves*

HORSE PROFILE
Country: Japan
Type: Pony **Height:** Around 12 hands
Colours: Usually black or seal brown
Personality: Tough, independent, gentle

WAR HORSES

From carrying soldiers into the heart of battle to pulling equipment and delivering medical supplies, millions of horses, ponies, mules and donkeys have played important roles in wars throughout history. Without the help of these faithful and courageous animals, many battles could not have been fought or won.

SADDLE UP

People didn't start riding horses into battle until around 800–900 BCE. This transformed the way people fought one another – a group of soldiers on horseback (called cavalry) was quicker and more powerful than a group of soldiers on foot.

The invention of the stirrup in China in around 300 CE gave soldiers greater stability in the saddle and allowed them to control their horses more easily on the battlefield.

An ancient people called the Scythians (you say it 'Sih-thee-uns') from Central Asia were some of the first people to use horses in battle (above). It's possible these fearsome fighters inspired the ancient Greek myth of the centaur (left), a creature that is part human, part horse.

CALL IN THE CAVALRY

In the medieval era (400–1400 CE), horses were essential to armies all over the world. Muslim soldiers in Asia and Africa used light horses to carry them swiftly into battle. In Europe, knights favoured heavy horses that could support the weight of their steel armour. However, the development of guns from the 14th century onwards meant that European armies stopped wearing heavy armour and switched to using faster, more agile breeds.

HORSES IN WORLD WAR I

Millions of horses and ponies took part in World War 1 (1914–1918), one of the biggest conflicts in human history. Many were civilian horses that had been bought by armies from farms, families, businesses and racing stables. Here are some of the ways these brave equines supported soldiers:

Cavalry – at the start of the war, thousands of troops on horseback were sent to the frontlines.

Ambulances – one of the most important jobs was pulling ambulance wagons. When roads had been destroyed or the terrain was so treacherous that motor vehicles couldn't get through, horses were vital for rescuing injured soldiers and delivering medical aid.

Transport and heavy lifting – horses, donkeys, mules and ponies were used throughout the war to carry ammunition, haul equipment and deliver supplies.

CARING FOR WAR HORSES

Without horses, armies on both sides wouldn't have been able to function, so special hospitals were set up to treat and care for injured horses. Even so, the frontline would have been a terrifying place for these animals. It is estimated that 8 million horses, ponies, mules and donkeys died from disease and injuries during World War I.

A special type of gas mask was developed for horses serving in the trenches to help protect them from poisonous gas attacks.

WARRIOR'S STORY

The life of a Thoroughbred called Warrior tells the story of millions of horses who served in World War I. Before the war, Warrior lived a peaceful life in the UK. He accompanied his owner, General Jack Seely, to the battlefront in 1914. Warrior carried Jack into some of the deadliest battles of the war, faced attacks from machine guns, and survived being buried in mud and being trapped in burning stables. Remarkably, both Warrior and Jack survived the war and returned home in 1918.

In 2014, Warrior was posthumously awarded the Dickin Medal, the highest award any animal can receive for bravery, in recognition of all animals that served in World War I.

AUSTRALIA AND NEW ZEALAND

There were no horses in Australia until the 18th century, when they were introduced by European colonisers. Similarly, the first horses to land in New Zealand set hoof on its islands in the early 19th century. These early horses were eventually used to create three Aussie all-rounders – a trusty riding pony, an agile light horse and a mighty heavy horse. A small population of horses also escaped into the Australian wilderness and New Zealand mountains, evolving into two unique feral breeds. If you need a tough friend to gallop through the Outback or a trusty pony to carry you stylishly around the show ring, you'll find them in this chapter.

Feral brumbies, shown here running free in the Australian countryside, have a problematic reputation. For many Indigenous Australians, the Brumby is a reminder of a time when European settlers arrived in the country and took Indigenous land. Large herds of free-roaming Brumbies can also damage wild habitats.

MĀORI HORSES

The Māori People of Aotearoa (New Zealand) first encountered horses in 1814, when British colonisers introduced the animals to the country. Horses were sometimes presented as gifts to Māori chiefs by settlers. As the number of horses grew, tribes started to buy their own. This established a rich tradition of Māori horsemanship that continues to this day.

KAIMANAWA HORSE
NEW ZEALAND

AUSTRALIA and NEW ZEALAND

AUSTRALIAN PONY

This dainty breed from Down Under has a fun, friendly character that reflects its Aussie heritage. The country's only pony breed, the Australian Pony was developed during the 19th century using breeds from Europe and Asia. These included Welsh Ponies (p42), Exmoors (p57), Thoroughbreds (p41), Hungarian Ponies and Timors (p97).

The Australian Pony has inherited the best traits of its ancestors and is very popular in its home country. It's an adaptable and robust breed that can be counted on to carry its rider over tough terrain in hot weather as well as proudly compete in the show ring. Australian Ponies can be used for all sorts of horsey activities, including dressage, driving competitions and gymkhanas.

These pretty ponies love to be groomed and made a fuss of, and make wonderful first ponies for children due to their affectionate natures – bring on the cuddles!

- Refined head with large, bright eyes
- Alert ears
- Powerful back
- Long, slightly curved neck
- Elegant, strong legs
- Neat hooves

HORSE PROFILE
Country: Australia
Type: Pony **Height:** 11–14 hands
Colours: Usually grey, but can be any solid colour
Personality: Affectionate, enthusiastic, reliable

AUSTRALIAN STOCK HORSE

The first horses to arrive in Australia were a mix of breeds, including Thoroughbreds (p41) and Spanish horses. Only the toughest survived the long voyage and, when they arrived, the challenging climate in their new home.

Over time, these horses were bred together to create a distinct type of light working horse. These horses were used on cattle ranches and as war horses, prized for their agility and endurance. This handsome breed was officially recognised and named the Australian Stock Horse in 1971.

HORSE PROFILE
Country: Australia
Type: Light **Height:** 15–16.2 hands
Colours: All solid colours
Personality: Hardy, adaptable, surefooted

AUSTRALIAN DRAUGHT

Many of the early European settlers in Australia were farmers, who travelled to the continent with their heavy horses in tow. Four breeds were particularly popular – Shires (p40), Clydesdales (p38), Suffolk Punches (p46) and Percherons (p50). These breeds were mixed together to create the Australian Draught.

HORSE PROFILE
Country: Australia
Type: Heavy **Height:** 16–17.2 hands
Colours: All solid colours
Personality: Strong, intelligent, sweet-natured

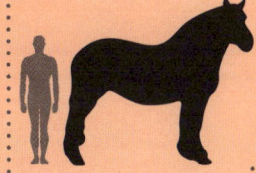

Reliable and kind-hearted, Australian Draughts were used to plough the land and pull wagons into town. A few small farms still use Australian Draughts, but most are bred today for horse shows or, sometimes, forestry work.

AUSTRALIA and NEW ZEALAND

BRUMBY

In the 19th century, European settlers flocked to Australia. Many came to mine the land for gold or build farms. Horses were essential companions – they carried people across the wild parts of the country called the Outback and hauled goods and equipment. But when farms failed or the gold ran out, the horses were often abandoned.

These horses became survival experts, thriving in habitats across the country – from harsh scrubland to remote mountain forests – and outwitting hunters who tried to capture them in attempts to control the number of feral horses. They came to be known as Brumbies and around 400,000 roam Australia today.

While some Australians celebrate these horses as an Australian breed, others see Brumbies as a problem. Because the horses have no natural predators, large herds can cause damage to the country's wild habitats. Various charities advocate for the humane control of Brumby numbers and run sanctuaries to care for them.

Straight head with big, intelligent eyes

Elegant neck

Short back

Very strong hooves

Slim but strong legs

HORSE PROFILE
Country: Australia **Type:** Light
Height: Varies but usually around 15 hands
Colours: All colours
Personality: Tough, intelligent, independent

Brumbies are free-spirited equines, but they can be tamed. As they are so at home in Australia's wild landscapes, they make excellent trail-riding horses.

KAIMANAWA HORSE

There were no horses in New Zealand until 1814, when a stallion and two mares arrived with British settlers. Early settlers used horses for farming and transport, and also presented them as gifts to the country's Indigenous Māori people.

By 1876, a herd of various breeds was spotted living wild in the Kaimanawa Mountains, a landscape of tussocky grasslands and jagged peaks in the country's North Island. It's thought these horses had been let loose by their European or Māori owners or escaped from sheep farms. Over time, they bred together to create a totally unique type of feral horse – the Kaimanawa.

Each year, these hardy horses are rounded up and around 200 are removed from the herd to be rehomed. This is done to control the number of horses living on the mountains, where endangered plants are found. When tamed, Kaimanawas can be trained for various events, such as showjumping and endurance, and make exceptionally loyal riding buddies.

- Large, expressive eyes
- Fairly short, strong back
- Thick mane and tail
- Short neck
- Tough hooves
- Muscular legs

HORSE PROFILE
Country: New Zealand **Type:** Light
Height: Usually around 15 hands (but can be as small as 12 hands or as tall as 16 hands)
Colours: Any coat colour
Personality: Tough, intelligent, intrepid

RECORD-BREAKING HORSES

As a horsey mega-fan you don't need to be told that horses are incredible animals – but do you know just how amazing they are? Read on to learn some astounding facts about our equine friends.

GENTLE GIANT

A Shire Horse called Sampson, from Bedfordshire, UK, was the tallest horse ever recorded. In 1850, he measured 21.25 hands (2.19 m, or 7 ft 2.5 in) high. Sampson was a giant even by Shire Horse standards – most male Shires are around 17 hands high. His owner believed Sampson was so tall thanks to his diet of oats and barley.

OLD BILLY

The title of 'oldest horse that ever lived' goes to Old Billy. Billy was a mixed breed (possibly a Cob and Shire Horse cross) who spent most of his life tugging barges along canals in central England. He was born in 1760 and died in 1822 at the grand old age of 62.

TINY BUT TOUGH

The smallest horse ever recorded was a miniature brown mare called Thumbelina, from Missouri, USA. Little Thumbelina was just 4.2 hands (44.5 cm, or 17.5 in) tall – roughly as big as an English bulldog. She may have been small, but Thumbelina had a big personality. Apparently, she thought nothing of escaping under fences and bossing around other, much bigger horses on her farm!

THE MANE EVENT

An American Paint Horse called JJS Summer Breeze holds the record for 'longest tail on a horse'. This horsey Rapunzel's long locks measure 3.81 m (12 ft 6 in). It takes her owner 3 hours to shampoo and brush Summer's tremendous tail.

SUPER SPEED

The speediest horse is a Thoroughbred called Winning Brew. She smashed horsey records in 2008, by reaching speeds of 70.76 km (43.97 miles) per hour in a two-furlong (402-m/1,320-ft) race held in the USA.

HIGH JUMPS

The highest jump ever recorded was 2.47 m (8 ft 1.25 in). It was jumped by a horse called Huaso ex-Faithful, in Santiago, Chile, on 5 February 1949. The highest jump by a miniature horse was 1.17 m (3 ft 10 in). This record was set in Bargemon, France, on 2 May 2020 by a miniature horse called Zephyr (shown here).

EQUINE EINSTEIN

A horse that can do maths?! A super-smart rescue horse called Lukas holds the record for the 'most numbers correctly identified by a horse in one minute'. Clever Lukas can identify 19 numbers (with his nose).

GLOSSARY

Breeding programme
The planned breeding of a group of animals. This helps to establish breeds that share similar characteristics or features.

Bridle
A set of straps put around a horse's head to help a rider control the horse's movements.

Canter
A three-beat gait. This means that the horse's feet move in a special pattern to create three beats: first one of the back feet moves (1st beat), then two diagonal feet move at the same time (2nd beat), and then the final front foot moves (3rd beat). A canter is faster than a trot, but slower than a gallop.

Colt
A young male horse, usually less than four years old.

Dickin Medal
A British medal awarded to an animal that has performed an act of great heroism.

Domestication
The process of taming a wild animal.

Double coat
A coat formed of two layers – a rough, weather-resistant topcoat and a soft, thick undercoat.

Dressage
A horse sport where a horse and its rider perform a series of particular movements, sometimes accompanied by music.

Driving
In general terms, when a horse, pony, donkey or mule pulls a cart or wagon. Driving is also a type of horse sport where a horse, or team of horses, pulls a two- or four-wheeled carriage.

Endangered
Refers to an animal that is at risk of disappearing forever from the wild forever.

Endurance riding
A horse sport where horses and their riders race outdoors over long distances.

Equine
A member of the horse family, or relating to horses.

Eventing
A horse sport where a horse and its rider compete across three events – cross-country, dressage and showjumping.

Farrier
A person who specialises in horse hoof care, including fitting horseshoes and trimming hooves.

Feathering
Long hairs that grow around the hooves of some breeds of horse and pony, such as Clydesdales.

Flaxen
A pale-yellow colour.

Foal
A baby horse.

Furlong
An old-fashioned imperial unit of distance equivalent to around 201 metres (220 yards). The term is still used in horse racing.

Gait
The pattern of leg movement that horses use to get around. Most horses have four natural gaits: walk, trot, canter and gallop. Some breeds, such as the Peruvian Paso and the Missouri Fox Trotter, have been bred to have special gaits.

Gallop
A fast, four-beat gait (meaning each foot moves independently). A full-on run.

Gymkhana
An event, usually for children, involving horse riding and jumping competitions.

Hand
An old-fashioned unit of measurement, which is still used today to measure horses. One hand is equal to 10.16 cm (4 inches). A horse's height is measured from the ground to its withers (the highest part of a horse's back).

Heavy horse
Large, strongly built breeds that have been bred to pull heavy loads. They are also known as draught horses. Examples of heavy breeds include the Shire, Percheron and Italian Heavy Draught.

Light horse
Slender breeds that have been bred mainly for riding and horse sports. Examples of light breeds include the Thoroughbred, Quarter Horse and Andalusian.

Mare
A female horse.

Mottle
A speckled pattern on a horse's coat.

Mount
A horse that you ride.

Pace
A two-beat gait. In the pace, the two feet on the same side of the horse move forward at the same time. Compare with a trot.

Pack horse
A horse (or pony, donkey or mule) used to carry loads on its back.

Pony
A small, stocky type of horse, usually below 14.2 hands high at the withers.

Ranch
A very large farm, typically in North America, South America and Australia, where horses (or other animals such as cows and sheep) are kept.

Savanna
A flat area of grassland, with few trees, usually found in tropical parts of the world.

Stallion
A male horse.

Steed
A horse that you ride.

Steppe
A large, flat area of dry grassland, typically in eastern Europe and Central Asia.

Stirrup
A metal frame or hoop that is attached to the saddle by a strap, for holding the rider's foot.

Stud farm
A farm where horses and ponies are bred.

Trail riding
Riding on off-road paths.

Trot
A two-beat gait where the two feet diagonally opposite each other move forward at the same time (compare to a pace). A trot is faster than a walk but slower than a canter.

Warmblood
An athletic type of horse, bred for sports, which often has Arab or Thoroughbred ancestry, plus some 'coldblood' heritage. *Coldblood* is another word for a heavy or draught horse.

Weaning
The process by which an animal stops being dependent on its mother's milk and starts eating solid food.

Withers
The highest part of a horse's back – from where a horse's height is measured.

Yearling
A young horse that is a year old.

INDEX

Africa 34, 60, 74–79, 80–81, 100
African wild asses 34, 80
Akhal-Tekes 7, 82, 89, 91
Algeria 74, 76
American Saddlebreds 15, 19, 21
American Shetlands 15, 18
American Standardbreds 15, 17, 51
Andalusian 26, 29, 32, 43, 58, 60, 61, 76
Appaloosas 11, 14, 18, 22
Arabs 6, 18, 21, 39, 41, 42, 48, 50, 53, 54, 55, 62, 63, 64, 66, 67, 70, 76, 77, 79, 82, 84, 86, 87, 88, 90, 91, 96
Ardennais 36, 52
Argentina 27, 30–31
Argentine Criollos 27, 30, 31, 33, 76
Argentine Polo Ponies 27, 31
Asia 6, 15, 31, 34, 69, 81, 82–83, 100, 104
Asian wild asses 81
Australia 102–106
Australian Draughts 102, 105
Australian Ponies 102, 104
Australian Stock Horses 102, 105
Austria 36, 55, 64
Azerbaijan 82, 86, 90

Bahrain 82, 88
Barbs 26, 32, 41, 60, 62, 63, 64, 74, 75, 76, 77, 78
Bashkir Curlies 14, 21
Basutos 74, 75, 79
Bataks 82, 97
Belgian Warmbloods 36, 49
Belgium 36, 38, 43, 49, 52
Bhirums 74, 77
Boerperds 75, 79
Boulonnais 36, 53
Brazil 26, 27, 32–33
breed (definition of) 7
Bretons 16, 36, 53, 62
Brumbies 57, 102, 103, 106
Budyonnys 82, 87
Burkina Faso 75

Camargues 57
Cameroon 74, 77
Campeiros 27, 33
Campolinas 26, 32
Canada 14, 15, 16, 22
Canadian Horses 15, 16
Cape Horses 79
Caribbean 29
Caspians 82, 89
Cayuse Indian Ponies 14, 22
Centaurs 100
chariot racing 59, 89
Chernomors 87
Chile 27, 29, 109
Chilean Horses 27, 29
China 68, 81, 82
Chincoteagues 56
Cleveland Bays 79
Clydesdales 7, 32, 36, 38, 39, 47, 85, 105
Colombia 26, 29
colours and markings 10–11

Connemara 36, 43
cowboys 14, 20, 26, 29, 30, 62
   see also gauchos
cross-country 32, 44, 63, 72, 85
Czechia 58, 59, 67, 71

Dartmoor Ponies 57
Denmark 36, 45
Dickin Medal, the 101
Dons 82, 85, 87
Dongolas 74, 75, 77
donkeys 6, 34–35, 46, 63, 65, 80, 81, 100, 101
dressage 23, 32, 42, 43, 44, 48, 49, 54, 55, 60, 61, 64, 66, 70, 71, 72, 73, 79, 87, 88, 104
driving 42, 61, 67, 71, 73, 104
Drum Horses 47
Dutch Warmbloods 72

Egypt 75
England 36, 40–41, 45, 46, 55, 57, 108
Eritrea 74, 77, 80
Ethiopia 80
Europe 15, 34, 36–37, 49, 58–59, 64, 66, 67, 68, 71, 88, 100, 104
eventing 55, 72, 79, 87
Exmoor Ponies 6, 57, 104

Falabellas 6, 27, 31
farm horses 7, 16, 19, 21, 23, 32, 33, 34, 35, 36, 37, 38, 42, 43, 45, 46, 49, 50, 52, 53, 54, 55, 61, 62, 63, 65, 67, 71, 74, 78, 85, 86, 97, 99, 105, 106, 107
farriers 13, 24, 102
feral horses 56–57, 103, 106–107
film horses 47, 58
Finland 36, 48
Finnish Horses 36, 48
Fjords 36, 45
Fleuves 74, 78
foals 6, 17, 18, 24–25, 55, 57, 93
France 16, 36, 43, 50–53, 57, 109
French Trotters 36, 51
Friesians 6, 11, 36, 37, 49, 54

gaits 19, 22, 28, 29, 32, 33, 44, 47, 94
Galicenos 14, 23
gauchos 26, 30
Gelderlander 49
Georgia 86
Germany 36, 54–55
Greece 59, 65
grooming 13
gymkhanas 104

Hackneys 18, 36, 41, 79
Haflingers 36, 55
Hanoverians 36, 48, 54, 55, 70
harness racing 17, 49, 73, 82, 84
Highland 36, 39
hinnies 34–35
hippogriffs 69
Hokkaido 82, 99
Holsteiners 32, 36, 37, 49, 54, 72
hooves 8, 9, 13, 92
horse and pony care 12–13

horse body language 92–93
horse racing 16, 17, 20, 22, 32, 41, 44, 48, 49, 51, 59, 73, 75, 78, 82, 84, 88, 89, 90, 91, 97, 109
horseball 73
horseshoes 13, 86
Hucul 59, 67
Hungary 59, 66–67

Iceland 36, 44
Icelandic 36, 43, 44, 57
India 81, 82, 94–95
Indigenous peoples of Australia and New Zealand 103, 107
Indigenous peoples of North America 14, 15, 22
Indigenous peoples of South America 27, 31
Indonesia 82, 96–97
Iran 82, 88, 89
Iraq 82, 88
Ireland 36, 43
Irish Draughts 36, 43
Irish Hobby 43
Italian Heavy Draughts 58, 62
Italy 55, 58, 59, 62–63

Japan 82, 98–99
Java 82, 97
Jennets 29, 32
Jutlands 36, 45

Kabardins 82, 83, 86, 87
Kaimanawa Horses 103, 107
Karabairs 82, 90, 91
Karabakhs 82, 86, 90
Kathiawari 82, 95
Kelpies 69
Kiso 82, 98
Kladruber 58, 59, 71
knights 40, 45, 50, 52, 100
Kuwait 82, 88

Lesotho 75, 79
Lipizzaners 58, 59, 64, 67
Lithuania 59, 70
Lokais 82, 91
Lusitanos 58, 61
Luxembourg 52

Mangalarga Marchadors 26, 32, 33
Maremmanos 59, 62
Marwaris 82, 94, 95
Mexico 14, 23
Missouri Fox Trotters 14, 21, 47
Mongolia 81, 82, 83, 91
Mongolian Horses 82, 83, 91
Morgans 15, 17, 19, 21
Morocco 74, 76
mules 6, 34–35, 46, 63, 65, 100, 101
Murgese 59, 63
Mustangs 21, 56
M'Bayar 74, 75, 78

Neapolitans 62, 63, 64
Netherlands, the 36, 38, 49
New Zealand 103, 107

Nigeria 74, 77
Nonius 59, 67
Norman Cob 16, 36, 50
North America 14–15, 20, 22
Norway 36, 44, 45

Oldenburger 36, 54
Olympic Games, the 51, 63, 70
Oman 82, 88
Orlov Trotters 82, 84, 85

palomino horses (definition of) 11
Pampa Horses 27, 33
Paso Finos 26, 29
Pegasus 69
Percherons 22, 36, 37, 46, 50, 85, 105
Peru 26, 28–29
Peruvian Pasos 26, 28, 29
Pindos 59, 65
pinto horses 11
Poland 59, 67, 70, 71
police horses 46, 62, 71, 95
Pony of the Americas 14, 18
Portugal 58, 61
Przewalski's horses 81
Puerto Rico 29

Qatar 88
qilin 68
qianlima 69
Quarter Horses 15, 18, 20, 76

ranches 14, 20, 28, 32, 56, 88, 105
rehoming centres 7
riding centres 7, 64
Rocky Mountain Horses 15, 19
rodeos 14, 20, 29, 30
Romania 59, 67
Russia 52, 59, 70, 81, 82, 84–87
Russian Saddle Horses 70

saddles 8, 18, 28, 75, 100
Salernos 58, 59, 63
Sandalwoods 82, 96
Saudi Arabia 82, 88
Scotland 36, 38–39
Selle Francais 36, 49, 51, 72
Senegal 74, 78
Shagya-Arabians 59, 66
Shetlands 8, 18, 31, 36, 37, 39
Shires 8, 36, 37, 38, 40, 45, 85, 105, 108
showjumping 32, 43, 44, 48, 49, 51, 54, 55, 63, 70, 71, 72, 87, 88, 107
Skyrians 57, 59, 65
Slovakia 59, 67
Slovenia 58, 59, 64
Somalia 80
Sorraias 58, 61
South Africa 74, 75, 79
South America 26–27, 28, 29, 31
Spain 23, 58, 60, 76
Spanish Riding School 64
Spitis 7, 82, 95
stables 13, 16, 24, 41, 51, 55, 60, 64, 101
stirrups 18, 100

Sudan 74, 77
Suffolk Punches 45, 46, 85, 105
Sumbas 82, 96
Sweden 36, 48
Swedish Warmbloods 36, 48

Tajikistan 81, 82, 90, 91
Tersks 82, 87, 91
therapy horses 17, 31, 47, 52, 55, 65, 98
Thoroughbreds 19, 21, 31, 34, 36, 37, 41, 42, 43, 46, 48, 49, 51, 53, 54, 55, 62, 63, 67, 70, 76, 79, 85, 87, 88, 91, 101, 104, 105, 109
Timors 82, 97, 104
Tokaras 82, 99
trail riding 19, 20, 28, 29, 30, 32, 55, 106
Trakehner 48, 55, 59, 70
Tunisia 74, 76
Turkmenistan 7, 82, 89

UAE 82, 88
Ukraine 59, 67, 70
Ukrainian Saddle Horse 59, 67, 70
unicorns 68, 69
USA 14, 15, 17–22, 23, 56, 108, 109
Uzbekistan 82, 90

vaccinations 25
vaulting 50, 73
Vladimirs 82, 85

Wales 36, 42
War Horse (film) 47
war horses 43, 45, 49, 52, 53, 61, 76, 79, 88, 94, 95, 100–101, 105
weaning 25
Welsh Cobs 36, 42
Welsh Mountain Ponies 18, 36, 37, 42, 57, 104
Wielkopolskis 59, 71

yearlings 25
Yemen 82, 88

zebras 80